Praise for *Resurrectic*

Some dreams come true, but others die a ... learn from both. In *Resurrection Year*, Sheridan Voysey writes from experience—there is life after the death of a dream. Your dream may be different, but the road to resurrection will be similar. I highly recommend it.

GARY CHAPMAN, AUTHOR OF *THE FIVE LOVE LANGUAGES*

This is a gentle, beautiful, deeply touching story of one couple who faced heartbreak but then asked God, "What next?" The result is a journey proving that, with God, our darkest experiences really can lead to new beginnings. *Resurrection Year* is a gift that will breathe life and hope into many who have faced a broken dream.

DARLENE ZSCHECH, SINGER, SONGWRITER,
WORSHIP LEADER, HILLSONG CHURCH

Gentleness, refreshment, and vulnerability are the delightful components of this wonderful book. Sheridan uses words and the gaps between words as an artist uses color and space to show rather than tell. We do not need to learn anything from *Resurrection Year* in order to enjoy it, but that is unlikely to happen. I am confident that it will change our hearts.

ADRIAN PLASS, AUTHOR OF MORE THAN THIRTY BOOKS
INCLUDING *THE SCARED DIARY OF ADRIAN PLASS*

This story of a crushed dream, a fresh overture, a reversal of roles, and a potent lesson on the emptiness of fame (like chocolate mousse—delicious, but merely air) seems sometimes akin to a travelogue. Sheridan's account of his and Merryn's struggle is helpful to those of us who couldn't have children, but the narrative compels us all to ask crucial questions about our visions and disappointments, our doubts and our prayers, our goals, purposes, and hopes. It is a profound read!

MARVA J. DAWN, THEOLOGIAN, SPEAKER, AND AUTHOR OF *JOY IN OUR WEAKNESS*, *BEING WELL WHEN WE'RE ILL*, AND *MY SOUL WAITS*

Resurrection Year is a beautifully written, honest, and engaging book that takes you on an emotional roller coaster through the reality of broken dreams and the wrestling that ensues. I will be buying copies for my friends who are living with dreams that haven't become reality.

ANDY FROST, SHARE JESUS INTERNATIONAL

This is a powerful and moving love story of one couple discovering how to love each other and God when their dreams are lost. The honesty and poetry of this memoir make it a compelling read, and will help many to find hope in dark times.

KRISH KANDIAH, EXECUTIVE DIRECTOR, CHURCHES IN MISSION, EVANGELICAL ALLIANCE UK, AND AUTHOR OF *HOME FOR GOOD: MAKING A DIFFERENCE FOR VULNERABLE CHILDREN*

Part autobiography, part prayer, and part apologetic, *Resurrection Year* is a tender and heartwarming book. Sheridan takes us on an intriguing journey through the perplexing maze of life, faith, loss, and hope. I really loved reading this book.

DEB HIRSCH, SPEAKER, COAUTHOR (WITH HUSBAND ALAN) OF *UNTAMED*, AND LEAD MINISTER OF TRIBE OF LOS ANGELES

I love Sheridan Voysey's honesty as he addresses the hard questions of faith. He lets us in on his pain to see how God works to stretch and grow him and his wife—and us. Sheridan offers no pat answers in *Resurrection Year*. His life illustrates the way God strengthens us in the struggle as we hold on to God even with our questions unanswered.

RUTH GRAHAM, AUTHOR OF *IN EVERY PEW SITS A BROKEN HEART*

This is not only a book for those with broken dreams, but equally a book for those whose dreams have been fulfilled but who still bear the responsibility to "bear one another's burdens and so fulfil the law of Christ." It calls all true followers of Jesus to empathize with those whose dreams are shattered and whose hopes are in limbo. It sounds remarkably like a conversation with Jesus.

REV DR. JOHN SMITH, MISSIOLOGIST, WRITER, PREACHER, AND
FOUNDER OF GOD'S SQUAD MOTORCYCLE OUTREACH

Through shades of vulnerability and pain, *Resurrection Year* offers new colors of optimism in this real-life story about hope and possibilities.

JOEL EDWARDS, INTERNATIONAL DIRECTOR, MICAH CHALLENGE

Resurrection Year is a wonderful, honest, moving book about loss, pain, and grief, but also about hope, faith, and above all love—the love between two people and the love of God. *Resurrection Year* reminds us all of a profound truth: in order for resurrection to happen, something has to die. This is a book for all who are struggling with loss and waiting in the darkness. There is hope, there is a dawn to come, there is resurrection.

NICK PAGE, AUTHOR OF *KINGDOM OF FOOLS* AND *THE WRONG MESSIAH*

Sheridan's writing is clean and edgy, sprinkled with the poetry of a heart that hears beyond the superficial to plumb the depths of grace. As he writes, despair and joy spring from the same place as this couple seek a way to live the truths of their faith and their love with authenticity. "Our world got so tiny," he writes, "our vision got so small—confined to the walls of our problems." What a powerful thought and one which has the capacity to lift our vision beyond the walls of our circumstances.

BEV MURRILL (MAGL), EXECUTIVE DIRECTOR, CHRISTIAN GROWTH
INTERNATIONAL; DIRECTOR, CHERISH UGANDA

Resurrection Year

Turning Broken Dreams Into New Beginnings

SHERIDAN VOYSEY

THOMAS NELSON
Since 1798

NASHVILLE   DALLAS   MEXICO CITY   RIO DE JANEIRO

Published in Nashville, Tennessee, by Thomas Nelson. Thomas Nelson is a registered trademark of Thomas Nelson, Inc.

Thomas Nelson, Inc. titles may be purchased in bulk for educational, business, fund-raising, or sales promotional use. For information, please e-mail *SpecialMarkets@ ThomasNelson.com*.

Library of Congress Cataloging-in-Publication Data is available upon request

ISBN 978-0-8499-6480-0

Printed in the United States of America

13 14 15 16 17 RRD 6 5 4 3 2 1

For Adrian and Bridget Plass—
who listened to us, listened to God,
and spoke a word in season

Contents

Author's Note

By the time we reach our twenties, most of us have a dream. We want to become someone—an actor, an artist, a mother, a sportsman, a builder, a teacher, a priest. We want to achieve something—perhaps make a movie or release a record, begin a social movement or build a church, compete for our country or start a business, write a book or simply have a happy marriage and family.

Dreams are the precious gift of our imagination. They create worlds that aren't yet real. They beckon us toward these worlds to inhabit them. And while there are some broad commonalities, our dreams are uniquely ours. The details of your dreams are not the details of mine. At their best, our dreams reflect our own potentialities.

When we are children, our dreams inspire drawings. When

we are teenagers, they keep us awake with excitement. As twenty-somethings, we start shaping our decisions by them, and by our thirties we may have seen some of them spring to life.

Or perhaps have seen some of them die.

You long to be married but are still single. Your artistic career has never taken off. A crushing diagnosis has shattered the dreams you held for your child. The whirlwind romance ended in divorce. As with our dreams, the details of our *broken* dreams may differ, but still they share some commonalities. There is sadness, a sense of unfairness, even jealousy toward those who have what we want. Life feels meaningless, we may battle feelings of failure, and we may harbor anger toward the God who has denied our requests.

But there is life after a dream has died. The God of the crucifixion is also the God of the resurrection. While a fairy tale cannot be promised (as there are precious few fairy tales outside Disney), the tragedy can make way for some joy. And while some scars will remain (as even Jesus carries the marks of his ordeal), healing and restoration can come.

Perhaps a greater tragedy than a broken dream is a life forever defined by it.

In anticipation of your own resurrection,

Sheridan Voysey

1

Ten Years in the Wilderness

December 24, 2010

Rain falls like a thousand bullets, a barrage of heavy drops pounding the roof, the hood, the asphalt. Windshield wipers on high-speed shovel away the deluge, yet the road ahead is a blur. Traffic has slowed to a snail's pace—six lanes of snails with little red brake lights banked up end-to-end, slowly creeping forward.

Australian summers are often like this—heavy, humid thunderstorms punctuating the blue skies and sunshine. But this season is different. The storms are heavier, darker, unrelenting. Roads will soon be washed away and whole towns evacuated. Floods will claim capital cities, regional centers, and lives.

Most of us are on our way to annual vacations and family reunions, to curious little faces eyeing little wrapped mysteries under tinsel-lined trees. In that sense Merryn and I are going against the tide, heading out of Brisbane, our families behind us, south to Sydney, to our little flat and some sanctuary.

Don't think, just drive. Turn the music up. No silence.

We'll stop halfway, in Coffs Harbour, at the same motel we'd stayed at on the way up just a few days before. Hopefully they'll have some room. Funny—here we are, a couple in transit on Christmas Eve, hoping there's room at the Inn.

"It's Christmas," I say to Merryn. "Let's try and get a Christmas pudding or something."

"You know there'll only be a microwave in the motel room," she says, her voice weary, her eyes red.

"I know." Dinner tonight will be basic.

The lights are still on at a large shopping complex on our left. We pull in and drive through the mostly vacant parking lot, getting a spot close to the entrance. Christmas muzak echoes off the glass and tiles inside. Roller doors are down and shops are shut, but the supermarket is open late. I slip my right hand into Merryn's and pick up a grocery basket with my left. "Let's find something nice," I say, trying to lift spirits.

"The Christmas puddings sold out days ago," the shelf-packer tells me. "But there might be some mince pies left in aisle 3." That aisle is almost barren, its wire racks holding little more than price tags and the odd busted carton of something-or-other. There are a few packets of mince pies, though. I put one in the basket.

"Let's just get some takeaway," Merryn says.

It's dark but the rain has eased as we walk back to the car, with our packet of mince pies and some bread rolls for tomorrow's drive. We get in, shut the doors, and Merryn bursts into tears.

"I feel so depressed," she whimpers.

A Chinese restaurant is open. The motel has a vacant room. We dump our bags on the floor and the food on the table. Merryn collapses on the bed and my heart breaks into a thousand pieces.

I pull out my journal and write:

God, this is cruel—leaving us in this wilderness. We've walked round in circles for years—tired, thirsty, and confused. One minute we've glimpsed the Promised Land, and the next minute you've barred us from entering it.

September 2000

She had loitered after lectures to get my attention. I had been taken by her smile and her laughter at my jokes. We had fallen in love in 1995, gotten engaged in 1996, and after getting our degrees and saying our vows before the congregation, had begun our life together in a two-man tent on a camping honeymoon that we'd never forget. Four years later we were in Perth, Western Australia, helping my fledgling radio career find its wings.

I walk into the kitchen. She's slicing cheese and putting it on crackers. The orange sun sets over the rise, a warm breeze flutters the curtains, and my radio station plays in the background.

"Honey," she says, "do you think we'll be here for a while?"

"In Perth?" I find a bottle of red in the pantry and pull out two wine glasses. "At least for the next few years, I'd imagine. Why?"

"We're starting to feel settled now, aren't we?" she adds.

"I think so," I say, wondering where this is leading. "Why?"

She pauses, then turns around to face me. "I think it's time."

"Time *for what* . . . ," I say slowly, apprehension building.

"To start a family."

I put the bottle down on the bench, draw a long breath, and exhale slowly. A flurry of thoughts invade:

Children. That means high chairs, baby food, nappy bags, the suburban life. Do I want this? Money. Will we have enough money? I'll have to change jobs. I've just started my career . . .

"You don't look too excited," she says.

Our marriage will suffer with kids—every marriage suffers with kids. No more date nights. No more sex. Merryn will start wearing comfortable shoes. I'll start wearing cardigans. I'm not ready for this.

"No, it's just that I . . ."

Listen to yourself. What selfishness. Why do you feel so apprehensive? What are you afraid of? Shouldn't you be happy about having a child?

"Wouldn't you like a little 'us'?" she says.

If my child gets teased at school, I'll walk right into that playground and deal with the bullies myself . . .

"I guess so. I'm just a little . . ."

"A little what?" she probes gently.

You're not cut out to be a father. You weren't much of a brother. You're too consumed with your work. You're not man enough to raise a son.

"Afraid," I admit.

She walks over and slides her arms around my waist. "We can face anything together, can't we?"

And by some miracle from above, by the end of the night I'm starting to get used to this fluttery feeling called expectation. We drink the wine and turn off the radio, leaving the curtains to curl and sway.

We can face anything together.

May 2001

Expectation, disappointment. Hope, then a letdown. The cycle is well known to many an expectant couple.

"It can take a few months to work," I remind her.

After six months the reminder wears thin.

"We need to get some tests done," she says.

June 2001

"You take it in."

"No, you take it in."

"I don't want to take it in."

"Well, *someone* has to take it in. Want me to ask that lady over there?" I point to a stranger walking down the footpath. "I'll just call her over . . ."

"No!" Merryn screams, and we sit in the car, giggling at our predicament.

A "sample" had been required for the medical tests, and we'd arranged a "home collection" to provide it. But that sample had needed immediate delivery to the clinic for analysis. Merryn cupped the yellow-capped specimen jar in her hand like a child holding a chick, keeping its precious contents safe and warm.

"This is ludicrous," she laughs. "What on earth do I say to the receptionist?"

I make a suggestion. "How about, 'This is a gift from my husband'?"

Without missing a beat she adds, "He sends it with all his love." We laugh hard.

Merryn carefully places the container in her bag, crosses the road to the clinic, and is back within minutes.

"We get the results in a fortnight," she tells me.

July 2001

The doctor sits quietly, his hands clasped and resting on the desk. Merryn stares vacantly at the lamp stand, and I search the floor for a knife to pierce the silence. Grey walls, grey blinds, grey chairs, grey files, grey papers, pens, plants, hearts.

"What about IVF?" Merryn asks, pulling a tissue from her handbag, her chin starting to quiver.

The doctor watches her for a moment, then glances at the file in front of him. "With these results, regular IVF won't be any help to you," he says. "The sperm count is just too low."

"So, that's it?" I say.

"No, there is one medical option open to you," he replies. "ICSI—Intracytoplasmic Sperm Injection. It's a form of IVF where a single sperm is injected into an egg in the lab to help it fertilize. The resulting embryo is then transferred into the uterus."

We fall silent for a while.

"There's always adoption," he says. "Although there aren't as many children coming through the system as there used to be."

I look at Merryn. The ground beneath her turns soft, her chair sinks into the carpet.

"Of course, some couples in your situation just choose to remain childless."

And Merryn quietly slips through the floor, into the bosom of the earth.

September 2002

What are we to be? Who will we become? Will we forever feel sad as we walk past a playground, with its parents and toddlers and games of tag? Will we feel isolated and envious as friends start their families, and will we lose touch as we live different lives? Will we feel lonely in our 40s, with our careers in full swing but with awards on the walls instead of drawings? And when old age hits, who will help us get dressed? Take us on outings? Listen to our mutterings?

January 2003

So many children around the world need a home. We

have a home. A child without a home finds a home without a child. Adoption has a biblical ring to it. But would the child ever feel like our child? And would Merryn ever feel like a real mum? Can you love a face that doesn't reflect your own? And can that face ever really love you back?

June 2003

Will we regret not giving IVF a try? Will we forever wonder what could have been? But the ethics of it all—creating all those embryos and discarding what isn't "needed." What about the taking of life? Are those embryos little lives? They say you can donate them, but with our genes in another woman's womb, whose child are they? And ICSI carries risks—possible complications. Could we cope with a special-needs child? Will we reap the effects of pushing nature too far?

Why can't we just conceive like everyone else, God? Even unwed teenagers are granted that.

Won't you heal me?

May 2004

The lounge room is warm and the company safe. Merryn and I sit on the couch as three angels minister to us. One is a businessman, another is a missionary, and the third a former nun. A heart for healing prayer is their common thread.

"Do you have a sense of faith about this?" the gentle nun asks us. "Any sense that God has promised you a child?"

We hadn't felt any such promise yet, we reply. But we believe in a God who heals.

"And so do we," says the businessman. They gather round us, lay their hands on our shoulders, and begin to pray silently, awaiting the Spirit's leading.

After a few moments the missionary speaks. "God, if there is any spiritual block to this pregnancy or anything hidden that you want to address, please reveal it."

And God steps into the room.

In an event that is as mysterious to me as it is shocking to Merryn, I begin to sob. And sob. And sob so deeply that I sometimes fight for breath. In eight years of marriage, Merryn has never seen me cry.

Our angels stay prayerful and the evening's course changes as subterranean feelings begin erupting within me: a sense of guilt over being a failure as a brother to my sibling; a sense of grief over what was lost and feelings of responsibility for it; the burden of expectations that I hadn't been able to meet; feelings of blame and regret I hardly realized had been there.

In truth, I'd never been keen on having children. As a teenager I'd even made a pact with myself not to have them, perhaps for reasons partly becoming clear. We break the pact and pray for healing—for a supernatural touch that medicine cannot equal.

I walk to the car exhausted but feeling a lightness of spirit. Something has changed within me. Something has been released.

Expectation . . .

June 2004

. . . followed by disappointment.

August 2004

The color is draining from her world. "Life seems so meaningless," she says. A career is a poor substitute for a family, although she might feel differently if she had a career she liked—something with purpose. And we're arguing a lot. She feels like her life is on hold until I resolve my IVF quandaries. I feel like she's pressuring me to make a quick decision on matters of life and death.

October 2004

The doctor says it's just a blob of tissue. The Christian doctors I ask avoid answering directly. "You're over-analyzing it," someone at church said. "My friend got a beautiful baby girl through IVF. Just do it." Before God, I can't use this technology if it destroys life. Yet no one will help me decide if it does or doesn't. Those ignorant of the procedure just want us to be happy, and those who know stay noncommittal. God isn't saying a word either way.

I feel so alone in this.

January 2005

"What do you dream of?" she asks me as we sit by the Swan River. Families congregate around barbeques like tribes around campfires. The park is filled with footballs and Frisbees, dogs and kites. Two boys on scooters race each other along the footpath.

"I want to write books, speak about God, and see that talk show idea come about," I say. They were the same dreams I'd shared a hundred times before, although notable in my answer was what it left absent.

"And what do you dream of?" I ask her quietly, already knowing the answer and feeling a stab of guilt for being the roadblock to its fulfillment.

"I don't know if I can have what I really want," she says. "But one day I would like to live overseas. Take a risk. Have an adventure."

July 2006

I slip my right hand into Merryn's and clutch the arm of the chair with my left. Merryn lies on the operating table in a white robe, a female doctor seated between her legs. An embryologist hovers in the background, and a computer monitor displays an ultrasound image of what is happening.

We live in Sydney now. My first book has been released. The talk show has become a reality. Merryn has started a new career, and we're shooting for a fourth fulfilled dream.

The doctor takes a thick, foot-long needle and pierces the vaginal wall. "Ow, ow, ow," Merryn says, gripping my hand.

"I'm afraid this *will* hurt a little," the doctor says empathetically. "The anesthetic only works so well." She pushes the needle deeper and into the right ovary.

"Argh!" Merryn cries in pain.

"There's the first one," says the embryologist. She's watching a screen and counting as each egg is extracted from the ovary.

But Merryn hasn't heard. Her heart rate has fallen and she's close to passing out. At the doctor's direction a nurse injects a vial of something into the IV line in Merryn's arm and her pulse steadies.

"There's number four," comes the embryologist's update.

The doctor repeats the procedure on the left ovary. "Ow . . . ," says Merryn groggily as the needle reenters.

Only six eggs are collected, but that, for us, isn't a bad thing. Our decision had been to fertilize a smaller number of eggs than normal and implant all the embryos that resulted, one by one. While this approach reduced our chances a little, it left our consciences settled.

Merryn is wheeled into recovery. An hour later the ICSI procedure has been performed and we are sitting in a taxi heading home. Merryn sleeps through the afternoon.

August 2006

"I've seen beautiful kids born from worse embryos than these," the doctor had said, trying to keep us buoyant. Only two embryos had emerged from the ICSI process, and due to their poor quality both had been implanted together.

Friends and family prayed night and day to the God of miracles. But such faith-fuelled expectation ends when the clinic calls with the results of the pregnancy test.

"I don't think I can go through that again," Merryn says as

we contemplate another round of IVF. "At least we tried," she adds somberly. "I won't wonder what might have been."

I drive to work. When I arrive, the producer of my radio show tells me she's pregnant.

March 2007

"And here," the new mother says, "is our little Jacob." She pulls her two-month-old out of the capsule and carefully hands him to Merryn.

"Hello there, little Jacob," Merryn says in that sing-song voice we all use with infants. "Aren't you a *cutie.*" Jacob scans the ceiling and hallway before finding Merryn's face and giving her a long stare. "Here I am," she says, opening and closing her eyes in an impromptu game of peak-a-boo. Jacob pokes his tongue through his lips a couple of times and wobbles his head in that jerky newborn way before nuzzling into her chest.

"I might need to feed him," Rachael says, smiling.

Like many of our friends, Matthew and Rachael are taking their first steps into parenthood. After Jacob gets a feed and is put down for a nap, we talk over lunch about sleepless nights and maternity leave, book deals and new careers. I'm grateful that baby matters don't dominate the conversation, and grateful that Merryn can happily hold someone else's child.

But later I find Merryn sitting on the bed, surrounded by scrunched-up tissues. "The only thing about having friends around with a baby," she says as I sit beside her, "is the reminder that we won't have one."

I hold her tight, wishing to heaven I could absorb her sorrow.

———

She pulls another tissue from the box and says to me, "Do you think we should consider adoption?"

July 2008

The social worker gathers her notes from our dining room table and readies herself to leave. "It's been so nice getting to know you both," she says. "I wish you the best of luck."

"So, we're done now?" I clarify. "There's nothing left to do?"

"I'll be recommending your approval first thing tomorrow," she says. "Then it's just a matter of waiting for the phone call."

The previous months have been hard. We've attended courses on both international and local adoption, and we've been shaken by the realities involved. Children in these programs arrive to their adoptive parents bruised by life, having languished in crowded orphanages, or having been born to drug-addicted mothers, or perhaps having been brought into the world as a result of rape. Some have been beaten and neglected, others are developmentally delayed, and some battle the effects of fetal alcohol syndrome or struggle with sadness and rage. Many will find it difficult to bond, fearing both rejection and intimacy. And some adopted children will then face racial abuse as they grow up in a new, foreign country.

This is our final meeting with the social worker who's been assigned to assess our suitability to adopt. Her interviews have been enjoyable but the application process has been harrowing. Having decided to adopt from within Australia, we'd needed to complete a form describing the kind of child we would accept. Would we take a child conceived by incest or born with HIV? What about one with epilepsy, Huntington's disease, or Hepatitis C? Would we take a child with a family history of schizophrenia, bipolar or another personality disorder? Would we take twins or siblings, or any nationality? Answering yes to many of these questions raised difficulties, while answering no felt cruel. And the more noes we gave, the more our chances of getting a child decreased. The exercise was designed to fit the right couple with the right child, but having never been parents, Merryn and I had no idea what our limits were. We talked, prayed, researched, and argued about a child we did not know with problems they may not have.

But as of tonight our application is complete—tucked in the handbag of the lady standing by our front door. While we know the wait could be long, theoretically we could be called to collect our child anytime.

The social worker pauses before leaving. "I probably shouldn't say this," she says, "but you'll be a very attractive couple to a birth mother wanting the best for her child. I don't think you'll be waiting long for that phone call."

September 2008
Could it be today?

October 2008
Mustn't get our hopes up.

November 2008
They said it could take a while.

———

December 2008

God, just lead us to the right child at the right time.

February 2009

There was a story on the news tonight—about a baby boy who was found on a conveyor belt at a western Sydney rubbish tip. He was only a few hours old when he was just . . . thrown away. A little life disposed of.

Merryn had to leave the room.

May 2009

We just have to be patient.

September 2009

One whole year and no phone call.

November 2009

Hope deferred makes the heart sick . . .

January 2010

Merryn's heart is sick.

"What can you really trust God for," she says through her tears, "when you ask with all your heart and you're ignored?"

June 2010

The sun sets on another Saturday as we sit at the table. So many dilemmas have been discussed and predicaments resolved here. This dining table is a place of laughter and hospitality, but also of struggle and turmoil.

"I read some journal articles yesterday," she tells me, "about some studies done on antioxidants." Merryn works in medical research, so I assume she's just making conversation.

"It looks like large doses of antioxidants can improve sperm DNA quality."

It only takes a second and I've collapsed inside, like an unplugged inflatable castle.

"You're not thinking about . . ."

"I guess I am," she replies, reaching for the tissue box.

"But we tried IVF," I say. "We tried it. Everyone prayed. It didn't work for us."

"I've always assumed it would be a waste of time trying again," she says. "But these studies . . . they show a *significant* improvement in male infertility after a course of antioxidants."

"By how much?" I ask.

"Up to 30 percent."

"Is that enough in my case?"

"It could be."

I put my elbows on the table and rest my head in my hands—a head that is now heavy with implications and ramifications. "But we've come this far with adoption," I say, my words tired. "Maybe the phone call is just around the corner."

"We've waited almost two years," Merryn says, tears running down her face, "and our lives have been on hold for even longer. I don't think I can take this anymore—this waiting, this uncertainty."

"And what if IVF is successful *and* we get the phone call?" I add.

"Given our luck so far, I can't see that happening," she says. "But even if it did . . . well, then we'd have *two* kids."

"And what about the trauma . . . ," I remind her.

"I could have a general anesthetic this time."

Silence falls across the table for a while as everything inside me screams. This torturous waiting, these anguished questions, the endless decisions, the unfairness of it all—I just want to go to sleep until it's over. But it's never over. It never seems to end.

"You really want to do this?" I ask.

"I think I do," she says.

"I've never wanted to hold you back from having a family," I say.

"I love you," she says, getting up from her chair.

We hug. And we pray.

June 2010

Merryn told the adoption agency about our IVF plans today. It turns out we can't continue with the adoption program if we do. We either abandon IVF or forfeit the progress we've made on adoption. It's all or nothing now.

July 7, 2010

Five eggs are collected. Three successfully fertilize. How many grow into healthy embryos will prove how much the cocktail of pills and powders I'm taking each day has worked.

Family and friends around the country are praying for us daily. I exercise faith and seek God expectantly:

Father, I ask for two things: that those three embryos grow strong and healthy, and that you bless us with a child from one of them. You are good and powerful. Just say the word and it will be done. I believe you for this. I trust you in this. In Jesus' name I pray. Amen.

July 12, 2010

Two of the embryos didn't make it, but one did. It was transferred today.

Please, God, give us a child.

July 23, 2010

Merryn's period was due two days ago. It's never been regular though, and the clinic says we shouldn't get our hopes up. Merryn has a pregnancy test this morning. We should know the answer by this afternoon.

Please, God.

Later, July 23, 2010

The clinic called. The test is inconclusive. Merryn's pregnancy hormone level is up but not by enough. It could be rising or falling. Another test has been booked for two days' time.

God, I still believe you can do this.

July 25, 2010

I sit in Sydney's Botanic Gardens, my journal in hand:

It has been said that God never lets you down.
But does he give you what you want?
When you've waited patiently after praying your
soul dry . . . ?
When all you can mutter in your exhaustion is Lord,
please . . . ?
And then this? Well, it can feel like he's let you
down.
Forgive me for being disappointed and angry with
you today, God. I'm sure it will all make sense one day.

August 2010

Another seven eggs. Four eggs successfully fertilized. Our best embryo transferred. And more disappointment.

I feel like I'm about to burst into tears all the time.
Perhaps I didn't pray enough, exercise faith enough,
oppose the devil enough. I can hardly pray at the
moment though. Feelings of spiritual failure haunt me.

September 2010

Merryn can't stop crying. "I don't know what to
hope for," she told me tonight. "I don't know what my
purpose in life is or what will make me happy. I feel like
I'll always be condemned to being restless and discontent,

wanting to be somewhere else without knowing where that somewhere else is."

God, why won't you come through for her? Why?

She's getting damaged by this.

Don't let her break.

October 2010

Merryn checks her phone. She has three voice mail messages from the clinic. She's already told them she won't be answering their calls at work today, so why do they keep ringing? Maybe this is important. Maybe they have news. Maybe this is . . .

"I'm sorry, but it's negative again," says the nurse.

"Oh," says Merryn before hanging up the phone.

She's decided to drop out of our church home group for a while. She doesn't want to talk about it anymore, as talk leads to tears and tears leave her weak. She no longer wants people praying for her either, as prayer leads to hope and hope keeps ending in heartbreak.

November 2010

"The Spirit of God has just come upon me," he says. "Can I pray for you?"

My Pentecostal friend John is one of the most caring guys I know. We're colleagues, and this sudden unction happens as we talk in my office, just three days away from Merryn and me transferring our final embryo. I readily accept the offer of prayer. John walks over, lays his hand on my head, and prays fervently—for protection of the embryo, for supernatural intervention in the IVF process, and for the creation of a healthy child. He ends his prayer with a blessing: "In the name of Jesus, may you be fruitful."

I thank John for his ministry. "It's been the prayers of others that have carried us," I tell him.

"Believe God for this," John says to me. "Believe God for this pregnancy."

And that's my problem, God. I can't believe with certainty that you will give us a child anymore. I've tried "believing", I've tried "exercising faith," and so far nothing's happened. Lord, I believe. Help me overcome my unbelief.

Anyway, what kind of God keeps us chasing him for ten years—doing special diets and fostering courses, waiting on adoption lists and suffering multiple IVF rounds, doing everything we can to honor you through it all, even limiting our options to protect life, praying daily and waiting patiently for you to grant us what so many receive easily—only to disqualify us from the prize at the end because we're too weak to "believe" for it?

Is that the kind of God you are?

Jesus, you healed a man lowered to you on a mat through a roof, not because of the sick man's faith but because of the faith of his friends.

If ours is lacking, at least reward the faith of our friends.

December 8, 2010

"Your pregnancy hormone level is 29," the nurse says.

Merryn swaps the phone to the other ear so I can listen in. "It's 29?" she says. "So that means . . ."

"That it's inconclusive again. We'll need you to come in for another test on Friday."

December 10, 2010

"If that hormone level has dropped, I'm not pregnant," Merryn says over breakfast, anticipating today's test. "And if it has doubled since Wednesday, I am. The level should double every two days."

Merryn calls me later at work. "The level is 45," she says.

"It's gone up . . ."

"But not by enough. The injections I'm having could be artificially inflating it. Another test is booked for Monday."

December 13, 2010

"They say I shouldn't get excited," Merryn says, crying down the phone, "but . . ."

"What's the level?"

"It's 160."

December 17, 2010

Our Friday begins with a blood test in the city, followed by breakfast at Darling Harbour. By ten o'clock we're back home, just in time for the phone call.

"It's Emily from the clinic," the voice says. Merryn puts

the call on loudspeaker so I can hear. "Listen, I've checked with another colleague here to be sure and . . ."

"*And . . .*" Merryn says expectantly.

"It's all looking good."

"It's looking . . . good?"

"Yes, it is. Your pregnancy hormone is at 450. It's caught up to where we'd expect it to be by now."

Merryn looks at me incredulously.

"We need you to have another blood test on Friday to work out when we stop your injections," Emily continues. "Then we'll do an ultrasound when you get back from your holidays."

"So," Merryn says, a little dazed, "it's all good?"

"It's all good," Emily replies, with a smile that shines down the phone line.

✲

Merryn hangs up the phone and stares at me, smiling. I stare back at her, feeling . . . numb. Or perhaps cautious. And after a moment I feel guilty for not feeling happy.

"I don't think we should get excited yet," I say to her, feeling every bit the wet blanket. "We've had too many false starts."

Merryn holds my hand tight.

"And besides, there's a good reason why couples wait three months before making the announcement. Too much can go wrong . . ."

"Emily said *it's all good,*" Merryn interrupts, trying to convince me.

"But she didn't say *You're pregnant*," I reply.

"Honey, we *are* pregnant! We've been pregnant for five-and-a-half weeks now. That's why the pregnancy hormone is so high." Tears start to well in her eyes. "We're going to have a baby," she says.

We call our families with the news. My mother squeals, cries, then squeals again. My Dad gives his great *Ha ha haaa!* laugh, the one reserved for victories. "I think I'm more excited for you two than for us," says my sister-in-law tearfully. Just two days before, she and my brother had announced they were expecting their second child.

We e-mail our praying friends. Within minutes text messages and e-mails fly back at us:

"I can't stop shaking with happiness!"

"I'm in the middle of the supermarket, bawling my eyes out!"

"God has answered our prayers!"

God, I whisper, *could it be? Have you finally answered our prayers?*

December 21, 2010

"Will you use cloth nappies or disposables? I'd go for disposables . . ."

"What car will you get? You'll need something bigger than that to fit a stroller in."

"Will you find out the sex? It will help when you buy clothes and choose colors for their room."

All was excitement the moment we arrived in Brisbane for Christmas. "You're going to be a daddy!" said my mother as she hugged me tight on her door step. My brother, his wife, and their daughter had already arrived, and the conversation soon centered on the joys and practicalities of our impending parenthood.

But while tongues of fire dance above their heads, Merryn and I are not graced with the spirit of elation. As much as we try, we can't enter their joy. I am still numb and Merryn is spent. The previous months have taken their toll, so we try to rest.

Perhaps the emotions will come tomorrow.

December 24, 2010

The next blood test is done nearby and the results are phoned through to the clinic. Emily calls around midday, and Merryn takes the phone outside for some privacy. A moment later she returns to our room.

She walks to the bed and lies down.

And curls up in a fetal position.

And that's when we pack our bags and drive—heading south, back to Sydney, with the windscreen wipers on high, dodging raindrops like bullets, with hearts as grey as the sky.

*

An ultrasound a few days later reveals that there had never been a baby. A gestational sac had been responsible for those pregnancy-like symptoms. While it should've housed a little body, it was empty. Even the doctors had been fooled.

Merryn doesn't cry when the doctor explains what has happened. She actually feels relieved. Hope deferred makes the heart sick, and prolonged uncertainty withers one away, but without hope perhaps the heart can now heal, and with some certainty perhaps the mind can rest.

"That was our last attempt at having a child," she tells the doctor.

"Oh," he says. "I'm sorry. That must be hard."

"Yes," we reply. "It's hard."

Ten years spent in the wilderness and no promised land.

———

2

A Consolation Prize and a Sacrifice

November 2010

The water is calm today in Five Dock Bay, its surface a shimmering sheet of cellophane. Cotton-ball clouds dot the deep-blue sky, and seagulls swoop as children toss chips in the air. Merryn and I walk along the Esplanade, near the jetty just past Taplin Park—still in the wilderness, our final IVF days ahead of us.

"There has to come a point," I say gently, "when we call an end to the journey."

"I know," Merryn says resignedly. "I can't keep doing this either."

I breathe a prayer of thanks that we're of one mind. Some couples try ten or twenty rounds of IVF in the frantic hope that the next attempt will succeed. Perhaps they have more emotional stamina than us.

"I think this should be our last round," she says.

"I agree," I say.

We turn onto Victoria Place and follow it to "the rock"—the nickname we've given our favorite spot on the peninsula. Look left from this cliff ledge and you view the Bay, with its bobbing sails and placid waters; look right and speed boats are racing up Parramatta River, leaving white foam trails stretching back to Sydney Harbour. Fishermen cast lines, kayakers paddle the shoreline, and when the sun sets the sky turns red and the western vista becomes a silhouette.

We sit on the rock, watching the water-lovers frolic. "If this really is our last chance to have a baby and it doesn't happen," Merryn says, "I need something else."

I've been watching a ferry pull up to the Chiswick pier but now turn to her.

"Our five years in Sydney have been all about having a family," she says. "If that doesn't happen, the thought of life going on as usual is just . . . it's just too depressing. I have to have something to look forward to—a consolation prize. Otherwise I feel like I have nothing."

I slip my arm around her shoulders, ready for the rescue. "What would you like to do, love?" I ask. "What would be a nice consolation prize for you?"

"I'd like to start again," she says. "Overseas."

Overseas.

"If we don't have a baby next year, could we move to Europe?"

*

She's never been much of a dreamer; never had grand aspirations as a teenager. She always assumed she'd get married, have some kids, and live happily forever after. Though she's now in the right career, a career for her was always secondary. Travel has been her only dream apart from a family — "Live overseas. Take a risk. Have an adventure," as she once told me. I can make that dream a reality — but only by saying good-bye to my own.

March 1994

The chair squeaks, my headphones are loose, and while everything is ready, I'm sweating. The music has been chosen, the tapes are cued, and all I have to do is press the button. My shaking hand hovers above the microphone switch. In 5, 4, 3, 2 seconds . . . I will talk on the radio for the first time.

This isn't the fulfillment of a long-held dream; I'd had no radio aspirations as a teenager. I sit in this chair quite by surprise—after an experience of divine guidance. When God found me, I was an eighteen-year-old searching for life among the flashing lights and throbbing beats of Brisbane's nightclubs.[1] Once found, I had prayed for two years to know what God would have me do with my life. The beginning of the answer came at church one night. A video was played during the service about a large overseas Christian broadcaster telling the world about Jesus. My heart began to pound. A week later I wrote to the Australian director of a similar radio network:

Dear John,

I'm not sure yet, but I think God might be calling me to work in radio. I don't have any experience in broadcasting, and I know I'll need some formal Bible training. Do you offer anything like that at your offices in Melbourne?

Yours sincerely,
Sheridan Voysey

I imagined my letter hitting the desk of a CEO running a giant organization with a multi-studio complex. I eagerly awaited John's reply.

As I waited something strange happened. Over the following days, two thoughts gently but persistently circled my mind:

Make contact with the Bible College of Queensland.

Get in touch with Family Radio.

I didn't know anything about the Bible College of Queensland. Perhaps someone had mentioned it to me somewhere. Family Radio was another matter. My father had turned it on in the car once—and I had soon hoped he'd turn it off.[2] Amateur announcers, dour-sounding preachers, and syrupy Christian songs were far removed from the strobe lights of my former world of nightclub DJ-ing.

Make contact with the Bible College of Queensland.
Get in touch with Family Radio.
Gentle. Persistent.
John's letter arrived two weeks later:

Dear Sheridan,

It's wonderful to hear what God is doing in your life. Actually, we're just a two-person office here in Melbourne, so I can't offer you any radio or Bible training. But if I were you, I would make contact with the Bible College of Queensland and get in touch with Family Radio.

Sincerely yours,
John Reeder

One fateful afternoon a couple of weeks later, I toured the Bible college campus and then met with Family Radio's manager. "You've got a good voice," the manager told me. "You should be an announcer." Until then I had assumed that any radio role I had would be behind the scenes, perhaps twiddling knobs in a recording booth somewhere. The thought of being on-air, speaking to thousands, was both thrilling and terrifying for this introvert, but I couldn't help feel that my calling was beginning to unfold.

I enrolled in college and practiced my radio skills at night when the station was off-air. A fellow student and commercial broadcaster named Fiona was teaching me. "You're sounding, umm . . . good," she had said, trying to stay positive after listening to my first practice tape. "Slow down a little and you won't make so many mistakes. And inflect down rather than up at the end of sentences. That way you won't sound like you're asking questions all the time." I had soaked up Fiona's advice, intent on never sounding amateurish again. "Oh, and don't pop your *P*s,' she'd added, noting the way I distorted words like *program* by leaning too close to the microphone.

It was Fiona who had found me in the college library just a few hours ago. "Sheridan, Paul has called in sick and Family Radio needs someone to do his show this afternoon. Here's your chance to go live!"

And so here I sit, with a lump in my throat and my forehead wet, waiting to say my first words to the masses. *You don't need to say much*, I tell myself, trying to stay calm. *You only need to string a few prerecorded programs together with some songs, not become Wolfman Jack.*

The intro music rolls and I press the mic switch with my quivering finger: "Welcome to the afternoon program," I say, popping the *P* of *program*. "My name is Sheridan Voysey," I add, inflecting the *zee* of my surname up high. "We-have-a-great-show-lined-up-for-you-today," I continue, the muscles tensing in my throat, pitching my voice high, and my words picking up speed like an over-caffeinated race caller, "including-Bible-teaching-from-Chuck-Swindoll's-Insight-for-Libbing—I-mean, Living—and-music-from-Davis-Meede-and-Gamy-Rant—I-mean, David-Meece-and-Amy-Grant. It's twelve-past-four—I mean, four-past-twelve."

And with those words, Brisbane is introduced to its newest radio host.

———

I stumble through the three-hour show, mispronouncing names and accidently ejecting CDs as they play, and after a deep breath and an embarrassed wave to the receptionist, I exit the station door and head for home, praying all the way for the gift of invisibility.

I don't think you're cut out for this, Sheridan.

A few days later a sweet lady in her sixties named Judy walks up to me at church. "Oh Sheridan," she says, "I heard you on Thursday. You have such a bright future ahead of you. I can't wait to see what God does with you next."

And I wonder if I shouldn't give up just yet.

December 1995

Little lights dot high-rise towers as office bodies clock-up overtime. Headlights streak along Coronation Drive as cars race out to the suburbs. The city's colors stripe the river in vertical bars, like the late-night test pattern on yesteryear's TVs. I sit on the ledge at Brisbane's Southbank, the Brisbane River sloshing by my feet, as couples wander the promenade behind me and the city before me bustles.

After nearly two years in that squeaky chair, I'm not popping my *P*s anymore or ejecting CDs mid-song. My inflections are about right, and I don't sweat anymore. I still chatter fast at times and stumble over my words. Ever the perfectionist, most weeks I still leave the station disheartened. But ever the angel, most Sundays sweet Judy has encouragement for me that seems sent from heaven. She's probably my only listener.

Over these past two years I've learned some nifty tricks—like how to talk over a song's intro, finishing my sentence just as the lyric starts. That's what announcers on the popular radio stations do. But what I've enjoyed most is learning to interview people. My first guest had been a local jazz singer. I'd felt so professional sitting in the foyer of the Holiday Inn on Roma Street, my tape recorder in hand, talking to her about lyrics and faith before she stood to sing. My second interviewee had been none other than Davis Meede—I mean, David Meece—who chatted to me past midnight after his 1994 show about forgiving his abusive father. David had sweated profusely and guzzled water continuously, and we had aimed every electric fan in our backstage room in his direction to help him recover from a strenuous performance in Brisbane's humidity. Through these experiences I have concluded that while playing music on the radio is OK, talking to people about their lives is where the fun is.

These are the thoughts I'm thinking when the chatter around me softens and the colors of the river fade. There by the river I slip into a fantasy world and begin to dream:

Imagine a radio show that interviewed authors, artists, and other interesting people about life and faith. Imagine a show where bands came to perform live and listeners called in to join the conversation. Imagine a show that reached the wider community, not just Christians. Imagine if that show aired live across the nation.

A child calls out to his friend and snaps me back to reality. This is a lofty dream for a radio wannabe at a tiny station with one old lady as his audience. But it makes my heart pound nevertheless.

———

June 2001

"It must be one long laugh-fest at your house," I say to my guest.

"Oh yeah," he says sarcastically, "one long laugh-fest. Some girls came up to my wife after I'd spoken at a meeting once. They said, 'It must be a laugh living with him.' And my wife said, 'Oh yeah. We get up in the morning and we have a laugh, we laugh over breakfast and we laugh over lunch, we have tea and have a laugh, and then we go to bed—and that's a real laugh!"

I'm in Perth now, hosting my first full-time morning show, and my guest is the British author, poet, and humorist Adrian Plass. Adrian has already regaled us with stories of incompetent hotel staff and unfortunate double entendres in church fund-raising letters, while passing on the profound wisdom of a clergyman who once warned folks not to become like South American Humming Birds (who, apparently, make a noise that sounds like *me, me, me, me*—get it?).

I'm having a ball.

This job is a gift. While I'm still playing music, the bulk of the station's interviews come to me. I've already spoken to renowned artist Pro Hart, *Phantom of the Opera* star Michael Crawford, and Olympic legends Shane Gould and Betty Cuthbert. International sports stars Justin Langer and Margaret Court, actors like *Get Smart*'s Barbara Feldon and Lois Maxwell from the *James Bond* films, and performers Andre Crouch and Stereophonics will soon join my growing guest list.

I ask Adrian about *The Horizontal Epistles of Andromeda Veal*, one of my favorite books of his, with its little girl protagonist who receives the fumbling help of churchgoers during a stint in the hospital.

"When I wrote that book, I had three sons," Adrian says, his tone a little more serious. "I never had any sisters or female cousins as I was growing up, so I desperately wanted a daughter. I think without realizing it I wrote myself one in Andromeda. I subsequently did have a daughter, Katie, who is an unsurpassed gift from God. But before she came I think Andromeda was my little girl."

I had a dream about my own little girl once—a literal dream, some years ago. She had straight blond hair, cut into a bob. She was looking at me over Merryn's shoulder. I wonder if she'll be a Katie or an Andromeda.

"I love the way," I say, "that Andromeda, throughout the story, gradually wakens to the idea that God loves her."

"I think that discovery is a gradual one for many of us," Adrian says. "For most of us it takes a lifetime to realize we're like kids walking through the playground holding our Daddy's hand—we can only see his knees. When I was converted at the age of sixteen, I knew everything there was to know about Christianity. Now that I'm fifty-two I know nothing. Except that I think there probably *is* a God and I think he's probably quite nice. What do you think, Sheridan?"

"Adrian, I think you're on the money," I quip, before cutting to a song.

Little do I realize, of course, how much Merryn's and my

own certainties will be challenged in the years ahead. Little do I realize how difficult trust in this "nice" God will become as our dreams struggle to be born.

But then again, little do I realize that each conversation in that studio is a step across the playground, God leading this kid toward a dream of his own.

June 2004

"So," he says, "where do you see yourself in five years' time?"

Jeff is the manager of a new radio station in Melbourne. We're sitting in an Italian restaurant around the corner from my Perth station. He's approached me with a job offer. A good one. It comes as I'm feeling restless and ready for change.

"Well, I feel like I've achieved all I can achieve here," I reply, a sentiment already known to my employers. During the five years I've been in Perth, my show's audience has grown significantly, and I've moved into middle management. I've been part of a major change in the station's sound, and my interviews are starting to air on other stations. "I've learned so much here."

"But?" Jeff says.

"I want to do more."

"Like what?"

I have learned a lot about myself in these past five years. I've developed a clearer sense of vocation. "I believe I'm called by God to be a writer, a speaker, and a broadcaster," I tell him. "So, if I'm going to be honest with you, in five years' time I'd like to be writing books, doing more public speaking, and hosting a radio talk show."

Jeff listens carefully, showing more of an interest in me as a person than as a potential employee, then says what is now obvious to both of us. "That doesn't sound like the job I'm offering you."

"No, it doesn't," I say, feeling foolish for having talked myself out of a good opportunity.

"But," he adds, "tell me more about this talk show idea."

I outline my Brisbane River dream: the authors and artists talking about life and faith, the live bands and talk-back broadcast across the nation. Even now the dream sounds naive. Christian radio has grown dramatically in the last few years, but there is nothing like this out there.

"I need to go," Jeff says, calling for the bill, "but we need to keep this conversation going. As it turns out, we have a similar dream for our station."

August 2004

I received three job offers this week. Word must have spread that I've resigned. But Merryn and I feel sure that none of them is for me—that I should take a faith step this time. I'm hardly an example of faith though. I worry; I fret; I lie awake at night anxious about the unknown. I feel like I've leapt across a chasm, unsure now if I'll reach the other side.

God, if I may, I ask you for that radio show.

April 2005

"Hi, Sheridan, it's Jeff. What have you been up to? Writing

---

a book? Good to hear it. When will it be in stores? November—just in time for Christmas. And what are your plans for the new year? Well I'm glad to hear that, because I want to talk to you about that radio show of yours. We're ready to do it, and the Sydney station is too. Which city would you like to move to?"

November 2005

This dream was never mine alone. Others have prayed for such a program too. When God wants something done, he gives the vision to many. We move to Sydney in January, where we'll see this dream come true.

8:59 p.m., April 2, 2006

I look around the studio. Everything is ready. My scripts sit neatly before me, and a blank computer screen sits ready for callers. My producer has our first guest prepared, and technicians are on hand in case of emergency. My chair doesn't squeak, my headphones fit, and those nervous feelings have become excitement.

The clock strikes nine o'clock, U2's *City of Blinding Lights* starts to play, and a female voice cuts across the music: "Around Australia, this is *Open House* with Sheridan Voysey."

I hit the microphone switch. "Welcome to *Open House!*" I say with a carefully rehearsed measure of controlled enthusiasm. "Every Sunday night from now, I'm hoping you'll be back. Consider *Open House* a place where you can visit with a few friends, interact with some great minds, get inspired for the week ahead, and explore life's questions."

Not a bad start, Sheridan.

"It was about ten years ago, sitting by the Brisbane River, that I first dreamed of a show like this. And looking at our list of guests and segments tonight, it feels like the dream has come true."

Good momentum so far.

"Australian cricket great Steve Waugh will be with us . . ."

So glad we got him.

" . . . plus author and poet Eugene Peterson."

This will be good.

"But I really want to hear from *you*. 1-300 40-20-20 is my number."

The U2 song swings back in and the show begins smoothly. Steve Waugh recounts the highs and lows of his sporting career and how meeting Mother Teresa inspired his humanitarian work. Eugene Peterson talks about his Bible translation, *The Message*; about mountain walks and daily prayer and his other spiritual practices. We hear from a charity serving the poor, talk to an anonymous West Papuan man seeking asylum, review the award-winning film *March of the Penguins*, and more. And the listeners start to call:

"I'm loving the show," says a girl in Sydney.

"We need more compassion for asylum seekers," says a man in Melbourne.

The artist Pro Hart has just passed away, and I play a snippet of our Perth interview in memoriam. I talk to a raceway chaplain about risk, a sexologist about singleness, and a caller named Dean about his favorite book, *The Seven Story Mountain*. The night has seriousness and humor, lightness and shade. When the show comes to an end, I'm tired but elated.

Tonight we were heard in Sydney and Melbourne. But in the months ahead the show will start to spread—first to country towns and then to almost every capital city in the nation. And the guest list will grow, as authors like Thomas Keneally, Mitch Albom, Anne Rice, and Marilynne Robinson, artists like Third Day, Jars of Clay, Marina Prior, and James Morrison, Christian figures like Joel Osteen, Tony Campolo, Mark Driscoll, and Max Lucado, and a bevy of thinkers, actors, politicians, and musicians join me to share their stories.

My producer and I review the night, and at 1:30 a.m. I pull out of the parking lot. I turn onto the highway and start slamming the steering wheel.

"Yes! Yes! Yes!" I shout.

Thank you, God. All of those years in Brisbane and Perth, all of the embarrassments and fumbles, all of that practice and sweet Judy's encouragements was all in preparation for this.

August 2006

"In 1967 a diving accident left Joni Eareckson Tada a quadriplegic. She's with us now on *Open House*. Joni, you must've asked yourself why God hasn't healed you."

"Oh my goodness," she says, "I went to so many faith healers. I got anointed by oil. I confessed my sins. I followed every single scriptural injunction. I had faith to the extent that I was calling my friends on the telephone and explaining to them that the next time they saw me they'd see me on my feet. I really was way out there on a limb with my confidence that Christ would heal me. But he didn't.

"Christians sometimes want to erase suffering out of the dictionary. If you read the Bible you will see that it is often God's best tool to make us more like Jesus. The choice is simply ours to yield to it and to allow him to use that suffering rather than complaining, avoiding it, escaping it, divorcing it—we've got all kinds of solutions for suffering except to embrace it as God's will for our life. But when we do, what a difference his grace makes."

September 2007

"Philip Yancey is my guest tonight. Philip, I've never seen you mention anything in your books about having children."

"That's because we don't have children," he says. "It would be hard to imagine life with children. I can barely get through a day as it is! We have lost, I'm sure, a lot of the joy and redis-covery of life that children bring. But we've gained too. We have gained by trying to use that time in other ways.

"I've talked to many people over the years who will have one thing that they wish was different. They might say, 'I wish I was married,' or 'I wish I had children,' or 'I wish I *didn't* have children.' I don't find a lot of help in dwelling on things that can't change. We seem fascinated by cause—why did this happen? The Bible doesn't really give us a lot of help on the issue of cause. In fact, it tends to switch the focus to our response: Now that it has happened, what are you going to do about it?"

December 2008

"We're talking to *Celebration of Discipline* author Richard Foster. What have been the most significant experiences shaping your life and work, Richard?"

"Well, I first want to talk a little about suffering," he says. "The first Bible verse I ever memorized wasn't John 3:16. It was 1 Peter 1:7: 'That the trial of your faith, being much more precious than of gold that perisheth, though it be tried with fire, might be found unto praise and honour and glory at the appearing of Jesus Christ.' The reason I memorized that verse was because my mother was dying at the time, and one of my first prayers was for her healing. It wasn't to be. She died, and a couple of years later my father died. And our little church community gathered around me and my brothers and became family to us.

"I think that one of the things we must learn how to do is suffer together. We are glad for all the wonderful medications and ways to relieve suffering today, but there are moments when we must go through difficult times together."

April 2009

While this infertility business is hard, other parts of life are exciting. My second book is out and doing well, and the publishers want a third. I have a keynote speech at Parliament House next month, addressing MPs and Senators. All kinds of people are calling the show— Muslims, Christians, sex workers, atheists. The load is exhausting at times, but I feel like God is using me. I feel like I've found my place.

March 2010

"Thanks for taking my call, Sheridan. I used to be a born-again Christian, but I'm an agnostic now. If there is a God, why don't more miracles happen?"

August 2010

"I haven't seen my children in twenty-one years. But having listened to your show tonight, I have hope again that one day I will find them."

October 2010

"I turned to prostitution to support myself and my kids. But this life is eating me away inside. I want to get out, and I want to find God again."

November 2010

"Adrian Plass, it's always a pleasure talking to you."

"Thank you," he says, and our interview ends.

It's been five years since my last conversation with Adrian, and almost ten years since our first back in Perth. This time I'm in Sydney, and Adrian is in North Yorkshire, but even a phone chat with Plass is gold to my audience. Our thirty-minute interview has roamed wide, covering life and loss, pain and faith, the gift of humor and the mysteries of God. Adrian has read some of his poems and we've had a few laughs. I stop the recording but we continue to talk.

"Tell me more about your move to North Yorkshire," I say.

"Bridget and I came here to help resurrect Scargill House,"

he replies. "It's a Christian retreat center that fell on hard times and had to close for a while. But it's coming good now. Have you been to the UK?"

"Yes, back in 2002 for a holiday."

"Well, if you ever come again you must visit us."

"That's very kind of you. Actually, Merryn and I have been, um, talking about travel."

"Really?"

And after some hesitation, I start telling Adrian about these last ten years in the wilderness. I share it all—the infertility diagnosis of 2001 and the IVF attempt of 2006; the adoption plans of 2008 and the horrors of the past few months. Adrian and I may have spoken a few times, but I can't yet claim him as a friend. I confide simply because he seems to care. And because he draws the story out of me. Because he listens.

"I don't know how it will work out," I add. "But next year has to be better for Merryn than this one. She needs a new beginning."

"In the Christian scheme of things," Adrian says, "new beginnings do come after the death of something, just as Jesus' resurrection followed his crucifixion. After what you've just told me, I think a resurrection year is just what Merryn needs."

December 2010

I close my satchel, swing it over my shoulder, say farewell to the few staff left at the venue, and step outside. Enmore Road is alive at one o'clock in the morning with merry revelers spilling out of Newtown's iconic pubs and clubs. I turn down Phillip

Street. The soft glow of the lampposts illuminates some of Sydney's finest street art—walls full of stencils, paste-ups, and mural-style graffiti. I find my car, unlock the door, throw my bag on the passenger seat, and fasten my seat belt.

But I don't drive anywhere. Instead I just sit there, staring blankly, before slumping my head on the steering wheel.

After ten years' wait it has to end so quickly?

The evening has been magical. Since *Open House* takes a break over January, our Christmas show each year is a celebration. Tonight hundreds of listeners had filled one of Newtown's music venues to see the show in action. Prominent guests had joined me onstage; singers had sung and bands had played. There'd been howls of laughter and moments of quiet, each interview guest bringing both humor and insight. In bohemian Newtown, with its street art and gay bars, we'd talked about a child born in Galilee who turned out to be a king. All the elements of my Brisbane River dream had been there—the authors and artists, the life and faith, the live performance and the national audience. My books had sold well too, staff told me.

Books. Speaking. Broadcasting. All I had once dreamed of I am now living.

And after just five years I am to relinquish it?

Leave all this and you start from scratch. If you give up the show you can't get it back. Publishers want authors with a "profile," so your future books may be in question too. You have no profile in Europe, and you have no contacts. In fact, what work will you do?

Sadness and adrenalin swirl like the purples and pinks of

those spray-painted walls. I know in my heart there is no other option. My ten-year dream may have been granted, but Merryn's ten-year dream looks set to be denied. I turn the key and start to drive.

I want Merryn to have that consolation prize.

3

Farewell to What Has Been

December 29, 2010

Her stare is vacant, her eyes are wide; we drive home from the clinic in silence. I compose the words of an e-mail in my mind, telling our rejoicing friends of our misfortune. *I should mention the ultrasound and the gestational sac and . . . Oh, I can't do this today,* I decide. Perhaps I'll tell them tomorrow, or the next day, when the sorrow subsides.

We park the car, dash through the rain, and climb the stairs to Flat 13. We close the door and bolt the lock, raising the drawbridge on life for a while. Home is a refuge, a hideaway, a sanctuary, a castle. We're safe within these walls from the world.

I fall onto the couch and stare at the coffee table. A pile

of letters sits unopened. From a large white envelope slips a powder-blue booklet. *Your Guide to Early Pregnancy*, it reads. An accompanying letter from the IVF clinic is dated a week earlier. "Congratulations on your positive pregnancy test!" it begins.

How cruel life can be.

Merryn is in the kitchen boiling the kettle. I walk in, lean on the bench, and look around the room. A high chair stands by the entrance, its tray in place and its harness ready. Next to it sits a pram, beside that rests a baby's car seat, and tucked in the corner is a fold-up stroller. In the fourth drawer down are bottles and feeding accessories. In the laundry, a patchwork play rug lies folded on the dryer.

There's a travel cot beneath our bed and a collection of children's books in the closet. On the top shelf of our wardrobe sits one of those electric mobiles that plays nursery rhymes as little toy animals twirl. It leans against the bright-red nappy bag. Just near the box of toddler's clothes.

They have come to us over the years as hand-me-downs and gifts, but now these items are symbols of loss—remnants of our wilderness journey, clinging to us like burrs on clothes after a forest walk.

God, what now? What next, and how?

Merryn comes in with the coffees, lies down on the couch, and starts reading a book. The cover says *Living and Working in Switzerland*.

December 30, 2010

"It needs to be fun," she says.

"And restful," I say.

"And full of adventure," she adds.

"With lots of beauty," I reply.

Our morning had begun with us trying to pray, but tears and sighs were all we could utter. We'd gone out to lunch, caught *The King's Speech* at the cinema, and by the afternoon were starting to feel a bit brighter. Rays of light had broken through the clouds as we'd settled into our fold-out chairs with a glass of wine on the balcony. Now we've begun to dream about the future—to make the first tentative sketches of what a Resurrection Year might entail.

"I feel dead inside," I say. "Lifeless. Numb. I want to get excited about something again. I want to resurrect my emotions."

"I want to resurrect my relationship with God," Merryn says. "He feels like an old friend who no longer returns my calls."

We sit quietly for a bit, staring into our wine glasses. With their bowls full and resting in our palms they almost look like crystal balls. But they give away no secrets.

"And you want to do this in Switzerland," I say.

"I really do," Merryn says, with eagerness in her voice that I haven't heard for some time. "One of the reasons I got into medical research was because of the travel opportunities, and there are plenty of positions I could apply for in Switzerland right now—I've been watching the job boards. Just imagine living in Geneva or Berne. Imagine doing hikes in the Alps every weekend. We could drive to Italy, Germany, or France, and England and Spain would only be a train trip away."

"That's true," I say.

"You'd have all the natural beauty your eyes could handle," she says. "Just imagine the photographs you could take."

I think of my shiny new SLR camera sitting in the wardrobe. It had cost me a small fortune a year or two back but had gone largely unused since. I hadn't had much energy for hobbies.

"And don't you think Switzerland would be an inspiring place to write your books?"

"I guess so," I say.

"So, what do you think? How do you feel about living in Switzerland?"

How do I feel? I feel like this whole damn thing is a curse. I feel like I'm too exhausted to move countries, but it's too late to stay. I feel mad at God for not coming through for us and sad at losing what I've worked for. I feel like frantically holding on to what I have left and curling up in a corner sleeping for a while. And I feel guilty—guilty for putting you through this when another man could've given you a family. And I feel like the last thing I could do right now is deny you what you so dearly want.

"I don't think I can get excited about anything at the moment," I say. "But I want you to be happy. And I like hearing you getting excited about something again."

Merryn reaches over and squeezes my hand.

"I'm so sorry," I say.

"For what?" she says, surprised.

"For being the cause of all this."

Tears well in Merryn's eyes. She puts down her glass, pulls her chair close, wraps her arms around my chest, and presses her cheek into mine. "You're the best husband a girl could want," she says. "Now let's leave the past behind and have an adventure together."

January 1, 2011

Goals for the New Year

1. Sell car (after cleaning it)
2. Sell washing machine (after final load)
3. Take excess clothes to charity shops (before selling the car)
4. Finish jobs in Sydney and find jobs in Switzerland
5. Get visas (to get to Switzerland to do the jobs)
6. Learn German (by May)
7. Plan a short holiday
8. Say farewell to loved ones
9. Get rid of baby stuff
10. Have a Resurrection Year

January 9, 2011

"I'll be sorry to see you leave," he says, "but you're doing the right thing."

Phil, my manager, and I sit in a coffee shop talking about my decision to leave *Open House*. We've worked through some of the technicalities involved and set March 27 as my final show. I'm glad to have Phil's blessing. He has been both manager and friend.

"Do you have any ideas for a replacement host?" I ask him. Phil throws me some names and we discuss each one. Some of them have considerable public profiles.

"There is one other option that I'll need to consider," Phil adds after a break in the conversation. "And that is closing the show altogether."

My face, no doubt, displays my surprise.

"The question will be whether listeners can warm to another host," he explains. "You've brought something unique to the role. The show has been shaped around you."

"But what if the new host brings more to *Open House* than I have? These are experienced people we're talking about."

"The show will still be different," he says. "*Open House* has been successful. If we can't find the right person to follow you, then I'd rather end it on a high than watch it slowly die after you leave."

And a little bit of *me* dies as he speaks.

January 15, 2011

I have these moments when it almost feels difficult to breathe—like I'm lying at the bottom of a deep pool, the weight of the water pressing upon me. That Open House could end is another weighty sadness. If I couldn't host it, I at least hoped it would live on. But Merryn and I prayed this morning. And it was as if I floated to the surface and heard the birds sing again. I felt like God might be in this move overseas, despite losing the show and despite my hesitancy.

Merryn's on the phone again, to another recruitment agency.

January 21, 2011

The door to the study opens and Merryn walks out to the lounge room. She's been on the phone to a recruiter about research jobs in Switzerland. The interviews have come thick and fast as Merryn's skills are in demand. Universities and pharmaceutical companies fight for the few medical statisticians there are in the world.

Merryn walks to the bookshelf by the front door, puts the cordless phone back in its cradle, and then sits down beside me.

"It isn't going to happen," she says.

I turn the TV off and face her. Her shoulders drop as she exhales a deep, disappointed breath.

"That's the seventh recruiter to tell me the same thing— that it's near impossible to get a visa to work in Switzerland if you're not European."

"But don't Swiss companies need people like you?" I ask.

"Yes, they do," she says, "but the country is notoriously tough when it comes to immigration. Visas aren't granted nationally— they're decided by each region, each 'canton.' And you can only work in the canton that issues your visa. One of the larger pharmaceutical companies occasionally applies for employee visas through its canton, but they're not always successful. And they have to prove to the government that they can't employ an EU citizen instead. Most companies just don't want the hassle of employing someone who doesn't already have a Swiss visa."

"I can get a British passport," I say. "Couldn't that help us?"

"Only if you were the one applying for the job," Merryn says. "And out of the two of us, I have a better chance of getting work in Switzerland." She's right. There aren't a lot of jobs going in Switzerland for radio hosts who don't speak German.

Merryn slumps forward, puts her elbows on her knees, and holds her head in her hands.

"A second dream dashed," she says.

January 22, 2011

"What do *you* want?" she asks as we sit on the balcony, sipping Saturday's sun.

"What do you mean?" I say.

"Well, so far this Resurrection Year idea has been all about what I want. But I want to know what *you* want. Where do *you* want to go?"

I pause for a moment before replying. While there have been no secrets between us—Merryn has known how I've felt about leaving Sydney all along—I've been careful not to hamper her hopes with my free-flowing feelings. The Resurrection Year *has* been about her, and for good reason.

"I know the beauty would've been amazing," I say, "and I know it would've been an inspiring place to write. But I never wanted to move to Switzerland."

"I know," she says.

"As our trips to the developing world have shown, I'm pretty inept at learning new languages. How many times did I mix up words in Haiti?"

"Well, it *was* funny when you greeted people saying, 'Toilet?'"

"So how would I have lived in a country that speaks four languages other than English? I could write books, sure. But not speak or broadcast. I would've lost two of the three things I do."

We had booked ourselves into an intensive German course that was to have begun this evening. But with last night's visa realization, and our lives already overwhelmed, we have decided to pull out. I'm miffed at losing the course fee, but relieved to forgo the linguistic torture.

"You know that I would rather stay in Sydney," I continue. "But whenever we pray about leaving, I do feel strangely peaceful about it."

"You couldn't get excited about Switzerland," Merryn says, "but could you get excited about another country?"

"Yes," I say.

"Where?"

"England."

Perhaps it was growing up with English parents. Perhaps it was flipping through their old photo albums. Perhaps it was hearing their memories of Cambridge and Chelsea, or the vague recollections I had of visiting grandparents on the Isle of Wight as a child. Wherever it came from, I'd always had affection for the United Kingdom and felt almost nostalgic for the country.

"Going to England isn't quite as romantic as going to Switzerland," Merryn says. "Remember how much it rained during our holiday there?"

"Grey skies aside," I say, "if we live in England we can easily

---

visit Switzerland. And France. And Germany. And all the other European countries you've always wanted to see. The UK is rich in history, it's full of natural beauty, and . . ."

"What?" Merryn says.

"The locals speak English."

"Not in the north they don't." We laugh, and the laughter feels good.

"We wouldn't have any trouble getting work visas for Britain," Merryn says, in a tone that suggests she's warming to the idea.

"And since I can also get British citizenship," I add, "we could stay as long as we liked—even relocate permanently if we wanted to."

We sit quietly for a while, sipping our coffees, our thoughts away in the clouds. Then Merryn gets up from her chair.

"What are you doing?" I ask.

"I'm going to search the job boards," she says. "I wonder if they need medical statisticians in the UK."

Later, January 22, 2011

"Take a look at this," she says, handing me a piece of paper.

Merryn has spent the past few hours online, combing through hundreds of job vacancies in Britain. She hands me a page fresh from the printer—a bullet-point list of selection criteria for a medical statistics position.

The list has two sections. I read the "Essential Skills and Experience" section first: Strong postgraduate qualifications. Fluency in study design and analysis. Substantial medical statistics experience, supported by a publication record.

"This looks promising," I say.

I read on to the "Desirable Skills and Experience" the employer is looking for: Specialist knowledge in clinical trials. Peer review of scientific papers. Experience in delivering medical statistics training.

"You tick all of these boxes," I say. "You could apply for this job in a second. Who's it with?"

Merryn breaks into a smile.

"Oxford University," she says.

February 4, 2011

"Good to see you again, Sheridan," he says as we shake hands.

"It's good to see you too, Leigh," I reply, leading my visitor from the radio station foyer to the boardroom.

As the host of a nationally televised news show, Leigh is a familiar face to many. He's spent decades in television and radio and has a résumé of high-profile scoops to his name.

"I'm sorry to hear you're leaving *Open House*," he says as we sit down at the shiny boardroom table. "I guess neither of us was expecting to have this conversation."

"No," I say, "this wasn't the way I imagined things working out."

"What happened?"

Leigh may be a big name in the media world, but he's also a man of faith, so I share a little of our wilderness story with him. Having faced some of life's harsher realities too—his career once interrupted by a lengthy illness—he can empathize. We dwell in each other's stories for a while, sharing a few lessons from the school of affliction.

"I was excited to get Phil's phone call," Leigh says as we move on to our meeting's purpose; "—sad to hear you were leaving but excited to be considered as a replacement host. I love what you've done with the show."

"We've worked hard at building a program that centers on faith but is credible to the mainstream mind," I say.

"Judging by the audience figures," he says, "I think you've achieved that."

"We explore the whole of life, not just a few pet topics," I add.

"Your *Life, Faith, and Culture* slogan sums that up perfectly," he replies.

"We take an invitational approach to Christianity—inviting people to see the world through faith-touched eyes, while giving those who disagree with us opportunity to say why."

"That's evident."

"And we need a host who will stay true to this original vision while taking the show to greater levels of influence."

The conversation moves to formats, editorial policies, topic choice, and guest selection. I recount some highlights of the show to date and areas where it needs improvement. Leigh scribbles in his notepad and offers some suggestions. Good ones. All of them.

I think we may have our new Open House *host.*

"If we were to pursue this further," Leigh says as we conclude our meeting, "there could be one barrier to my taking the role."

"What would that be?" I ask.

"My current employer. My contract doesn't allow for additional media work outside of the company. They may be sympathetic to the idea, or . . ."

"They may not," I say.

"Right."

We walk back to the foyer and say our farewells. I then proceed up the hallway, turning into Phil's office.

"We need to pray," I tell him.

March 2, 2011

" . . . in Jesus' name, Amen."

Merryn gets up from the couch, walks into the study, closes the door behind her, and waits. In a few moments the phone will ring and four voices from Oxford University will test her suitability to work at one of the world's most prestigious institutions. While we've prayed about the phone call, the butterflies flutter in Merryn's belly.

The phone rings.

The interview begins.

"In a subgroup analysis," a quickly spoken man asks after some administrative chat, "how would you determine if the treatment effect was different in one subgroup compared to the other?"

Merryn thinks for a moment. "Well," she says, "you would include an interaction term in your model, between the treatment variable and the subgroup variable. So the model would be: treatment-plus-subgroup-plus-treatment-by-subgroup interaction."

"OK, thanks," he says.

Did I miss something? Merryn wonders. *The question seems too simple and my answer feels too short. Will they tell me if I answer correctly or not?* The butterflies grow restless.

A sixtyish woman with precise pronunciation asks the next question. "If you were asked to calculate a sample size for a study with a nonparametric analysis," she says, "how would you go about doing it?"

A nonparametric sample size calculation? Merryn thinks. *I only know about parametric sample size calculations. Oh heck, I don't know the answer.* The butterflies start to swarm.

"I'm actually not sure," Merryn says.

"The answer," the woman intones, "is that you would transform the data, if possible, or bootstrap a confidence interval."

Beads of sweat break on Merryn's forehead. Sydney's summer nights can be balmy, and the room is now considerably warm. She tries opening a window but the phone cable won't let her reach the latch. The butterflies are now ramming her insides.

"A doctor wants to develop a risk model to predict thirty-day mortality," the man says, his speech fast. "He's collected data on 150 patients and has forty variables that are possible predictors. How would you help him develop the risk model?"

"You said 150 patients and forty predictor variables?" Merryn clarifies, reaching for paper and pen. "How many events were observed?"

"There were fifty deaths," Gary says, "so that's 33 percent of the data."

"First," Merryn says, her confidence rising, "thirty-day mortality is a binary endpoint, so I'd fit some form of logistic regression model. Secondly, forty candidate predictors is far too many for this amount of data, so I'd reduce that."

"And how would you determine if your model was good at classifying patients?"

"I could calculate the discrimination c-statistic, or plot observed events against expected events by . . ."

"OK," he says, "that's fine."

Another question follows, and another—this one settling the butterflies, that one sending them into a frenzy. Merryn stumbles out of the study an hour and a quarter later, exhausted from the violence wrought on her insides.

"How did it go?" I ask in cheery ignorance.

"Terribly," she says, collapsing onto the bed. "It was like taking a masters-level statistics exam on the phone in a sauna."

"But how well did you answer the questions?" I ask.

"I nailed some of them, I waffled through others, and some I have no idea whether I answered well or not. The panel gave little away."

"When do they decide on the position?"

"Sometime next week," she says. "But I'm not getting my hopes up."

March 3, 2011

People ask me what my plans are. I don't know what to tell them. I've always been so driven, but now everything is unknown. We've booked our plane tickets though. England is a given. If no work opens up, we can always come home. God, what is your next assignment for me, and what is it for Merryn? And will Open House continue with a new host?

March 4, 2011

My desk phone rings. "Can you come and see me," Phil says. I walk around to his office and close the door behind me.

"I've just spoken to Leigh," he says, "who has just met with his management."

I wait for his next words.

"They've released him to work with us," Phil says. "*Open House* will continue, with Leigh as its new host."

Later, March 4, 2011

My mobile phone rings. "It's me," Merryn says. I walk into an empty studio and close the door for privacy.

"I just got an e-mail from the Oxford University panel," she says.

"Already?" I say, excitedly.

"Want me to read it to you?"

"Yes, read it."

"Are you sure?"

"Go on, tell me what they said."

"I can always wait until you get home . . ."

"Get on with it!"

"'We are pleased to offer you the position of medical statistician at Oxford University's Centre for Statistics in Medicine.'"

"Oh, love . . ."

"Honey, we're going to Oxford!"

*

Merryn is so excited. As it turns out, she'll be working with a world-renowned professor in the medical statistics field. This is such an unexpected turn of events, and Oxford is such a beautiful city to move to.

God, you do come up with surprises sometimes, don't you?

March 27, 2011

"And now," I say to the audience, "the moment you've been waiting for—the unveiling of the new host of *Open House*."

I sit in a black leather chair on a constructed stage with bright lights in my eyes and a lively crowd before me. The radio station courtyard is our venue and the night sky our canopy. Waiters serve the crowd, technicians mix the sound, and thousands listen in as I relinquish the show I love. The name of my replacement has been kept a secret until now.

It's an emotional night. Some of the show's regular guests have surprised me with farewell gifts, which, they joke, reflect my personality. To the audience's amusement, one gift is the TV series *Mad Men* and another, a weighty tome called *Philosophical Foundations for a Christian Worldview*. Soon the laughter of such moments will turn to tears as singer Andy Sorenson speaks for the first time about his childhood sexual abuse, then performs a song announcing his return to public life.

My producer, Clare, has arranged some listeners to share what *Open House* has meant to them, and it is their words that nearly break my composure:

"After university I was feeling hopeless. I started listening to your show every moment I could, and I found hope again. I want to thank you for that."

"Time and again, Sheridan, I've been blown away by the empathy you've shown to your guests and callers and the way you've opened your life to them."

"I'm not a Christian, but as I've listened to you each Sunday, you've really made me think. So often I've felt this warm feeling from you and the Christian community."

"Your show has gotten me through some very difficult times. Although I've never met you personally, I feel like I'm losing a friend."

Your kind words hurt, friends. Your kind words hurt tonight.

"He has met the Queen," I continue, introducing my successor, "and has covered tens of thousands of stories, ranging from the death of John Lennon to the attacks of September 11. You'll know him best as a news anchor—formerly with Channel Seven and currently with Sky News Australia. And now you're about to know him as the new host of *Open House*."

Recognition flickers on some of the crowd's faces.

"Ladies and gentlemen, would you please welcome journalist, broadcaster, author—Leigh Hatcher."

The crowd erupts in applause as Leigh walks onto the stage. We shake hands, the cameras flash, then we take our seats to chat.

I have one goal for the next few minutes—to help *Open House* listeners warm to Leigh. They may have known him as a journalist or a news anchor, but not yet as someone to share their deepest hopes and doubts with. After recapping his illustrious career, I move to the story that will help build this bond.

"Tell us about your season of illness," I say.

"I was midway through my holidays in 1998," Leigh explains, "and I came down with a virus that anyone could've contracted. It began my two-year battle with chronic fatigue syndrome. I was a high-profile journalist at the time, and I lost my job. I was in the midst of a busy speaking ministry at churches, and I lost that too. The physical pain was one thing, but I still can't believe I was unemployed for two years."

"Two years is a long time," I say.

"It is," Leigh replies. "I lost a lot through that season, but I gained a lot too."

"Like what?"

"Anyone who goes through pain," he says reflectively, "will realize at some stage that the experience has been character-building. For me, the greatest change came in regards to my faith."

The crowd sits silent, listening.

"I had lots of head knowledge about God," Leigh says. "I had even taken a year off work just before my illness to do theological study. But as my wife and I went through this journey of loss, I came to *know* that God was true. That's a different thing than believing in God because someone has preached to you, or because you've read it in a book. Through pain I came to know God was there, personally. He was with me, through it all."

. . . with me, through it all.

"So much of my life, my faith, my career, and even my journey of illness," Leigh adds, changing tack slightly, "comes to a completion in this great task of hosting *Open House*. And I want to pay a formal tribute to you, Sheridan, and the work you've done. This show is unique in broadcasting, and it is a privilege for me to take it on, but only because you, under God, have built such a wonderful foundation for it."

The crowd applauds. I feel both affirmation and agony. That a man of Leigh's stature would feel this way about hosting my little show reveals the hand of God. But the sense of loss is still weighty.

"I have one final question for you," I say to Leigh as the applause dies down.

He looks at me, ready.

"Consider *Open House* as my daughter," I say, "and me as her protective father. What are your intentions with my little girl?"

The crowd roars with laughter.

"I'll be good to her!" Leigh assures me before sharing his future plans for the show. And as more singers take to the stage and the show comes to a close, the proverbial daughter is handed over to begin her life with another. I climb down from my chair, pose for a few shots, shake a few hands, and sign a few books. The full reason for my leaving is never told, revealed only in the knowing looks of our nearest and closest.

There'd been a standing ovation at the end. Darlene Zschech had sent a farewell message, as had other church and political leaders. They'd all make nice memories.

Memories. I can take the memories with me. Memories of

singer Gloria Gaynor telling me how the emptiness of fame had gotten her searching for God, and of former Nixon aid Charles Colson describing his role in the Watergate affair. Memories of activist Shane Claiborne throwing money to the poor at New York's Stock Exchange, and of Andrew White, the "vicar of Baghdad," telling me about the four-million-dollar bounty on his head. Memories of one-time gang leader Nicky Cruz in tears, recalling how Jesus changed his life, and of author Bryce Courtenay spontaneously singing the song he'd sung as his son died in his arms.

Memories. I can keep the memories.

I give my producer Clare a hug and she cries.

And I drive home.

March 28, 2011

"Last night was your last *Open House* show?" he says.

"Yes," I say.

"For good?"

"For good."

I'm sitting in a cafe on Sussex Street with an executive from a major publishing house. He'd been impressed with my books' sales figures and had made contact some months ago. Someone had recognized me in the elevator of his company's high-rise, impressing him further. Publishing a book with him would be significant.

"Will you be out of radio for long?" he asks.

"I really don't know," I say. "Things are up in the air for me at present."

"I hope you can recoup that audience somehow," he advises. "Us publishers . . ."

" . . . want authors with a profile," I say.

"It's the nature of the business right now."

March 29, 2011

Insignificant, unimportant, no longer relevant, yesterday's man.

Feeling low, earlier than I expected.

April 2011

"Are you happy for me to throw this out?" she says.

Merryn stands at the door, holding the item under discussion. I sit on the study floor, two giant piles of books teetering beside me.

"Absolutely not," I reply.

"And why?" she asks.

"Because that is a family heirloom," I say. "It must come with us."

"Honey."

"What?"

"It's an egg cup."

"Yes, it's an egg cup," I say incredulously, "—just an orange plastic egg cup to you. But it's an orange plastic egg cup that I made myself, as a thirteen-year-old in school." Some people have no sense of nostalgia.

"What about this then?" she says, ducking into the kitchen and returning with another item.

———

"You want to throw away my chrome-plated egg flip too?"

"You made it in metalwork class," she says. "Your dad got it chromed for you, and it sat on your shelf as an ornament afterward. That's weird in itself. It's never even flipped an egg."

"It didn't need to. I used the egg cup, didn't I?"

"It looks like you're making progress," Merryn says, surveying the scene around me.

"I certainly am," I say proudly.

"Let me guess," she says, "—this is the pile of books you want to take to the UK, and this is the pile you're going to give away?"

"Not exactly."

"Well, what's this pile?" she says, pointing to the three hundred-odd books on my left.

"That's the 'take' pile."

"And this one?" she says, pointing right.

"That's the 'undecided' pile."

"You can't take them all!"

"Of course not," I say calmly. "The 'leaving' pile is over there." I point to a third stack of books in the corner. Merryn eyes it up and down.

"There are seven books in that pile," she says.

"I know. And I'm in two minds about the Yancey book. Maybe I should keep it."

Merryn groans, then walks back to the living room, where she's culling the contents of dusty storage boxes. Tired and thirsty from the thankless task of rereading my library to choose each book's destiny, I come through a little later in search of water.

"Remember this?" she says, holding up an old, battered saucepan.

"Indeed I do," I say wistfully.

Black on the bottom from countless flames and scratched from steel wool scrubs, the dented pot had been our sole cooking implement during our first months of marriage. We'd been penniless students when we'd walked down the aisle, lacking funds for an exotic honeymoon. But we had a '74 Corona and a two-person tent, and a window of opportunity without mortgage or pets, so we took off for an adventure of driving and camping, cooking one-pot meals in that saucepan.

Two-minute noodles were easy enough, and mum's tuna-spaghetti dish worked a treat. But two-stage cooking on a single-burner stove put these domestic amateurs to the test. Many a dinner was cold, others were half-cooked, and a container load of pepper fell into one fateful dinner when the cap of the shaker fell off.

The saucepan's lid had soon lost its handle, but we'd improvised with a champagne cork. And with that old, battered saucepan we'd had the time of our lives: driving from Binna-Burra to Byron Bay, from Scotts Head to Sydney, from Canberra through to Melbourne and along the Great Ocean Road, before heading home via Wagga Wagga, pulling into Brisbane two months later.

"Good times," she says.

"Good times," I say. That cork-handled saucepan was full of memories.

"But please don't tell me you want to take it to England," she says.

"No, it's time for that one to go."

Merryn places the saucepan on a growing pile of goods near the front door. Another mound of stuff sits beside it.

"What's that pile?" I ask.

"This is the junk pile," she says.

"And the other one?"

"That's the charity-store pile." On the top sits an orange plastic egg cup and a chrome-plated egg flip.

"At least they'll bring joy to someone else," I say.

"I'm sure they will, dear," Merryn says with a strange smile on her face. "I'm sure they will."

April 2011

"I'm calling about the washing machine and whether it's still for sale . . ."

"I saw your bookshelves on eBay and wonder if you'd consider making a deal . . ."

"Your advertisement is now live. Your car will remain online until it sells . . ."

✳

"Your visa has been approved and will be delivered within seven working days . . ."

"Your relocation is confirmed for Tuesday, May 10. Our movers will arrive by 9:00 a.m. . . ."

"I have a tenant for your apartment with good references. I'll drop the paperwork in for you to sign . . ."

*

"You've both meant a lot to us. This church won't feel the same without you . . ."

"Can you squeeze us in on Saturday? We'd love to see you before you go . . ."

"Dear friends, please join us at the Golden Century Restaurant on Friday to say farewell to our beloved Sheridan and Merryn. They've never tried Peking Duck before. We can't let them leave until they do."

*

"I think that's all of it," Merryn says, pushing a bright red bag into the last available space.

Merryn steps away as my sister-in-law closes the door. Kristy's car is full to overflowing.

The folded-down pram had just fit into the trunk, leaving some room on top for the stroller. The high chair is on the back seat, beneath the children's books and travel cot; the baby's seat is wedged behind the driver. The bottles are in a box on the floor, underneath the bright red diaper bag. The electric mobile is on the passenger's seat, resting safely on the play rug, and bags of bibs and jumpsuits have been pushed into the spaces left over.

"Thank you," Kristy says. "This will all be so useful."

"I'm glad," Merryn says.

"We'll see you on Monday, before you leave?" Kristy confirms.

"We're looking forward to it."

Kristy brushes a hand over her baby bump before getting into the car. The car pulls off and turns up the street, and as Merryn waves, all the reminders of our wilderness are carried away. A fresh breeze sweeps in from the bay, and the burs that once clung are plucked from Merryn one by one.

No more high chairs in the kitchen.

No more travel cots under the bed.

No more children's books in the closet.

No more. Farewell.

Farewell to the reminders, the remnants, and the symbols. Farewell to the dashed hopes that made the heart sick. Farewell to the heartache, the cruel twists, and heartbreak.

Farewell to the broken dream.

Farewell to what has been.

May 18, 2011

We slide into our seats, clasp our belts across our laps, look each other in the eye, and smile.

After months of sorting, selling, donating, and packing; after weeks of finalizing bills and winding up accounts; after streams of strangers collecting our belongings, and nail-biting moments as cars almost fail to sell, we are now here. Sitting on a plane. Setting off from home. Beginning the adventure. Leaving all we know behind.

The stewards begin their safety routine as the plane pulls away from the terminal.

The past few days have been hectic. I have flown to Adelaide and back to fulfill a speaking engagement, and to the Gold Coast before that to receive a broadcasting award. After a flurry of fare-well dinners and coffees in Sydney, we had traveled to Brisbane to say good-bye to family, where there were lunches, laughs, tears and hugs, and endless games of hide-and-seek with the nieces. We'll miss those little girls. Our brothers and sisters too. Our parents will be waving from Departures right now.

The plane begins to taxi down the runway.

And now we head to a new and distant land—a land of castles and cathedrals, old pubs and rowing clubs, of Big Ben and Stonehenge, the Cotswolds and the Highlands; the land of Chaucer and Austen, Shakespeare and Milton, Wordsworth and Dickens, the Brontes and Blyton; the land that gave us tennis and cricket, Monty Python and Sherlock, Pink Floyd, Coldplay, Bacon, Chaplin, and Hitchcock, plus Wesley and the Methodists, Booth and the Salvationists, Wilberforce and the abolitionists, and a thousand brilliant minds.

We turn into position, ready for takeoff.

And our new city, Oxford—how exciting it will be. A city of ancient towers and "dreaming spires," of writing, thinking, and learning; the city of C. S. Lewis, J. R. R. Tolkien, Lewis Carroll and W. H. Auden, Dorothy Sayers, Oscar Wilde, Graham Greene, and Philip Larkin; a city of political battles and famous sermons, of prime ministers' educations and George Whitfield's conver-sion; a city of beauty, history, creativity, and inspiration—this is the next city we will call home.

The engines roar, the plane shakes, and we are powerfully thrust down the tarmac. Our wheels leave the earth and we climb into the air—lifting to the heavens, lifted to resurrection.

And the higher we rise the smaller our old life becomes— the airport is soon miniaturized, its parked planes like children's toys. Higher we climb now, higher and higher—the city's high-rises like Jenga stacks and its houses like Lego blocks. Up into the clouds we fly, whiter and whiter, before breaking through the misty pillow to the infinite blue beyond.

Our old life is but a speck.

We look at each other and smile.

Let the Resurrection Year begin.

4

Resurrection Begins in Rome

May 19, 2011

Bubbles, bubbles everywhere—soft, shimmering, translucent. Balls of delight floating gently in the air—with little faces staring in amazement. A young man hoping for spare change works his tricks like a magician—his magic wand a couple of sticks looped with rope, his top hat a bucket of soapy water, his white dove a giant bubble flying into the sky. He soon draws a crowd in the piazza.

A little boy watches in wide-eyed wonder as one of these transparent beauties hovers. It is large enough to pick him up and carry him away, but rises and falls like a feather. At just the right moment the boy gives a shout and jumps up to touch the bubble. It bursts like a party balloon pricked with a pin, showering the boy with suds as he giggles.

Another bubble floats through and a girl rushes toward it, but she retreats when she realizes its speed. She winces as the bubble pops over her head, splashing her and the pavement with lather.

A girl in a yellow top can no longer resist. She's been filming the fun on her camcorder but throws that to her mother so she can join in. A bubble as wide as she is high hangs just before her. She pretends to carry it in her arms before exploding it with a finger.

Another boy rushes in to play, followed by a fourth child, and a fifth—a flurry of smiles and squeals breaking out on a sidewalk filled with sparkling spheres.

The children run and jump and reach to the sky, chasing and popping the bubbles. Free of reservations, constraints, and inhibitions, they enjoy the present moment, reveling in their excitement, delighting in the gift of bubbly, soapy play.

Their happiness is contagious, spreading like pollen in the breeze. They are playful. They are joyful. They are free.

And so are we.

✳

We decided to have a holiday on our way to England—two weeks in Italy and two weeks in Switzerland. Now Merryn and I skip down the cobblestone street, our eyes as wide as a bubble-chasing child. We have thirty-six hours to spend in the Eternal City. Our Resurrection Year has begun—in the grand city of Rome.

We had arrived in the city at midday, a shuttle bus dropping us at our little hotel. After following the signs down a maze of hallways and dragging our bags up a series of stairwells, we'd found Reception through a secluded doorway. Down another corridor we'd gone, descending a narrow spiral staircase before finding our old-fashioned key unlocked a thick wooden door that granted entry into our room on the second floor. It had white walls, mahogany-framed windows, antique-style furniture, and an arched red-brick ceiling.

"You like?" I'd enquired.

"I love," she'd replied.

We had asked the nice hotel manager behind the tiny reception desk to recommend a moderately priced restaurant for lunch. Following his hand-scribbled map through the backstreets and alleys, we'd found the spot, but not before passing delis full of cheeses, olives, meats, and breads, cafés bulging with panini, biscotti, pizzelle, and cannoli, and pizzerias tantalizing us with their doughy oregano scents. We'd taken our seats, ordered risotto and ravioli, and were soon planning ahead to panna cotta for sweets.

"Let's have some wine," she'd added.

"And coffee," I'd said.

Wine. Coffee. We'd had little of both for months, switching to fruit juice and decaf during each IVF round. And our dining table at home had been filled with supplements—zinc, selenium, folic acid, vitamins and antioxidants—a cocktail of colorful pills taken each morning in an effort to improve our chances of conception. But those days were over. The pills and potions were gone. Wine and coffee were back on the menu. We could eat whatever we wanted now.

With cups empty and appetites sated, we'd turned with excitement down the Via Nazionale, skipping past its hotels and classical-style buildings, heading toward the Piazza Venezia and our must-see sights. We'd taken the stairs at the end, near the Santissimo Nome di Maria church, passed Trajan's Column, and crossed the street. And now we stand gazing into the sky.

The *Il Vittoriano* monument is nothing if not grand. Made of gleaming white marble, replete with fountains and flags, this "altar to the nation" towers high above the city. A cascade of steps takes you to its first grand level, where the Goddess Rome stands central and an elaborately carved wall depicts victorious heroes and citizens. Above the Goddess, up another cascade of stairs, sits an immortalized Victor Emmanuel—the first king of a unified Italy, astride his horse, upon a pedestal. Ascending higher still, where the air gets thin, a row of Corinthian columns soar into the heavens. On top of them, seemingly miles away, sits two sculptures of the Goddess Victoria, galloping triumphant in her horse-drawn chariot.

The *Il Vittoriano* is both loved and loathed by Rome's locals. Some call it the "wedding cake" in jest. It has been described as the epitome of self-important architecture. But standing before the *Il Vittoriano* is a sublime experience. One feels small in its gargantuan presence and reminded of a larger reality by its grandeur.

———

"I think we go this way," Merryn says as we leave the monument.

"Are you sure?" I say. "Back that way looks more direct."

"Well, you try reading this map. I can't make heads or tails of it."

We'd had little time to research Rome before leaving home, and our travel guides had proven too heavy for our bag allowance. So, we try navigating the city using a free tourist map that is hardly to scale. We walk up one street, walk back a few minutes later, and pursue another road for a while before I encourage Merryn to take an enticing pathway that leads us on a roundabout trip of backstreets and alleyways.

"There it is, *finally*," Merryn says after thirty minutes of wandering.

"I told you this was a more direct way," I say, smiling.

We head toward the milling crowds, buy tickets from a spruiker, and, after waiting in line, pass through an archway to enter the mammoth structure. Its elliptical walls, nearly two millennia old, are grey and pocked with holes. We wind our way through the crumbling arcades, past columns, plinths, and pilasters, and climb the worn steps to the sun-soaked upper level of one of the world's greatest wonders—the Colosseum.

A tour guide tells us the stadium once held over fifty thousand people. We imagine yesteryear's Romans taking their places in the tiered seats and the spectacles they came to see. Some were brutal—bloody gladiatorial battles where slaves fought to the death, and gruesome animal hunts where beasts tore each other to shreds. But other attractions proved more humane.

Mythic tales were dramatized here with actors, props, and sets. Trees were planted in the amphitheatre's floor to create simulated forests for Rome's urbanites. History even records the arena being filled with water and battleships reenacting the great sea wars. Caesars were hailed here. Popes later prayed here. Christian martyrs stood on these stones. Contemplating this brings a sense of awe.

After a rest in the shade of Constantine's Arch, we turn down the Via Sacra and enter the Roman Forum—the political and religious soul of the once-great Roman Empire. The ruins of ancient temples and palaces surround us, echoing with mythic and historic tales. Romulus and Remus, the legendary twins at the heart of Rome's history, are said to have been raised by a she-wolf on the nearby Palentine Hill. To our right is the Rostra where the great orator Cicero spoke and Marc Antony gave his speech at the funeral of Julius Caesar. And just ahead, past the Temple of Saturn, stands an orange-walled building on the side of the hill. Only later do we discover that it's the Mamertine Prison. There, a sixty-two-year-old missionary once sat chained in its dungeon, writing a letter to his friend. "Do your best to come to me quickly, Timothy," he had written, knowing his life was at its end. The apostle Paul was the missionary, and Second Timothy was the letter. Before his martyrdom, Paul had spent his final moments here.

Marble monuments with stairs to the sky and battleships floating in stadiums; Caesars, Ciceros, and ancient remains; great saints of the faith and famous legends—such wonders have a curious effect on us. As we walk and look, muse and marvel, we are lifted out of our little lives. Immersed as we are in this history of humanity, our eyes are opened to a larger reality—an existence that seems wider and deeper than before.

Our world got so tiny, our vision got so small—confined to the walls of our problems.

For us it was an IVF clinic, an adoption office, a dining room table full of pills. For others it's a law court, a singles' site, or a curtained-off bed in a hospital ward. Those facing trials know how life can soon revolve around a particular room or place. And soon our world is reduced to those four walls, even when we walk out the door—our minds consumed with our longed-for, begged-for, not-yet-existent wish. Our world gets tiny. Our vision gets small. Everyday blessings are missed. We see the pixel and not the picture, the thorn and not the flower, the pebble and not the vista.

But life is much bigger.

It's late by the time we make it back to the hotel. We climb the various stairwells, trudge the many corridors, unlock the thick wooden door with our old-fashioned key, and collapse on the bed, exhausted.

"Wow," she says, staring blankly at the ceiling.

"Wow," I say, reflecting on the day.

Although it's late, the summer sun is still high. I drag myself from the bed to unlatch the shuttered window, falling back onto the mattress as a mild breeze cools our sweaty bodies. We lie still for a few minutes side-by-side before the sweet sound of an accordion sails into the room. A saxophone joins the melody. Then a male tenor starts to sing. Our serenade comes from street musicians beneath our window, entertaining patrons in the café below.

I reach over and squeeze Merryn's hand. She looks at me with an incredulous smile.

And we laugh like a couple of kids bursting bubbles in the piazza.

*

The morning light shines on their faces, causing a halo-like effect when viewed from behind. We join the throng along the Via Porta Angelica, the crowd a mix of many races. There are Italians, Asians, some brightly dressed Africans, and a little Indian girl who smiles at me over her father's shoulder. A couple of young nuns pass by, their faces as bright as their veils. We all walk into the light toward St Peter's Basilica.

How many are tourists and how many are pilgrims? I wonder as I look around at the stream of people. *And which of the two are we?*

A sermon is on my mind this morning—a sermon of my own. I had preached it in our church before leaving Sydney. It was on God calling Abraham to leave his home and travel to an unknown land. In it I'd made the point that God calls all of us at times to such journeys. I'd said that we, like Abraham, may only discover the destination once we begin walking, and that through such adventures God changes our identities. In a sense, then, this path toward the Vatican *is* part of a pilgrimage for us: A search for restoration. A journey of resurrection. We've left all that we know and are now in between homes, ready for God to change us along the way.

But with cameras in our hands and a bag full of snacks, we are very much tourists too. As we walk between the marble columns of the right-hand colonnade and step into Saint Peter's Square, our sightseeing instincts go into effect. Merryn photographs the obelisk, the Basilica's facade, and some of the 140 statues peering down from the balustrades, while I capture the subtle details—an old man engrossed in his newspaper, a *carabiniere* making his rounds, a nun in a reflective pose watching the crowds.

My camera—that much neglected camera—feels so good in my hands. Peter Berger, the sociologist, has said that playful pursuits like hobbies give us a glimpse of heaven because through them we enter a timeless, joyful state. I savor that taste of the eternal again. To frame, focus, and capture an image is both an opportunity to do art and to meditate.

"I can helpa you skipa da lines," says a well-tanned man in a blue shirt, pointing to the long queue in front of the church. "Three-hour tour of da Vatican galleries," he adds in his thick accent. "Straighta through the gates—no wait."

"How much?" I ask.

"Thirty-five Euro each."

"We've been offered twenty," I say, having fielded three such offers already.

"You wanna my kids to go hungry?"

"No, I certainly don't want that," I say, but I start to walk away.

"OK, deal!"

Our blue-shirted ticket seller whisks us around to a group assembled by the Vatican Museum's entrance. Donned with headsets to hear the tour guide's commentary, we make our way through the turnstiles and security.

Nine miles of galleries. Thousands of pieces of art. Priceless sculptures, frescoes, and paintings. To walk along these ornate corridors is to be baptized in beauty. From the Room of the Muses with its fine sculptures of poets and deities, to the Gallery of Tapestries with its sixteenth-century drapes depicting the life of Jesus in Raphael-style imagery, the place is awash with splendor.

This is no less true of the Gallery of Maps, where a collective gasp is uttered by each wave of visitors passing through. My gaze is on the red and gold ceiling, with its dazzling images and filigree patterns. A gallery in itself, each inch of its 393-foot-long surface is filled with paintings, as if hundreds of little picture frames had been glued end to end. Merryn is drawn to the walls, filled with forty topographical maps of Italy. Painted in the sixteenth-century, long before the invention of aeroplanes, the bird's-eye-view frescoes of each region and city are remarkable in their detail, including streams, springs, castles, and ships.

How differently we understand the world, she muses, *the more of it we are able to see.*

We enter the dim, cavernous building of the Sistine Chapel. Hundreds cram between the walls, making the space hot and muggy, and despite the officials' continued calls for silence, the murmurs of the crowd echo into a loud, impervious hum. When our eyes adjust to the light, we begin to see the famous frescoes reprinted in so many art books: the life of Moses depicted on the left-hand wall, the life of Christ portrayed on the right, and Michelangelo's epic ceiling murals sixty-five feet up. In the center of the ceiling sits God, his finger famously outstretched toward Adam's, while surrounding panels depict a tree, a serpent, and the expulsion from Eden. On the altar wall at the chapel's far end is Michelangelo's crowning achievement—"The Last Judgment." Jesus has come, the angels are blowing their trumpets, the dead are rising from their graves, and heaven is just moments away.

As the ticket seller promised, we are soon at the Basilica's portico, having bypassed the spiraling queues. We walk up the steps, then step through the doors into St Peter's gargantuan nave. Over a third of a mile of marble floor stretches before us, inlaid with elaborate mosaics. The golden stucco vault soars fifteen stories high, and statues of saints as tall as houses lean out from each wall. The gilded bronze baldachin above the Papal Altar is a mass of swirling columns and cherubs, and behind it the golden Altar of the Throne proclaims the glory of God with its resplendent glowing center.

A man kneels at a confession booth. A woman lights a candle across the aisle. A pilgrim touches the worn foot of Saint Peter's bronze statue. And I wonder what is happening for others in the Basilica—what lies behind their somber looks or smiles. Within each of us is a world of joys, struggles, doubts, and questions. I wonder how many walk through these doors today searching for light, for absolution, or, like us, for restoration.

———

Saint Peter's bones are said to be buried beneath our feet, brought here after his own crucifixion. As the stone-carved martyrs around us testify, for now the glories of the world intertwine with suffering and trial. But one day this will not be so. One day the angels will blow their trumpets and he who defeated death will wipe each tearful face dry.

And until then one of God's good gifts to us is artistic beauty. *Refreshing, soul-lifting, worship-inspiring beauty.*

For while the art we've seen has come from human hands, the talent behind them comes from elsewhere: from the Spirit who hovered as the earth was taking shape; the Holy Spirit who inspired the artists of old.[1] Viewing such creativity renews my soul, giving me a glimpse of the Creator's face.

A ray of light bursts across the cathedral. I try to capture its effects with a series of photographs. Merryn waits patiently on a seat nearby as this beauty-loving romantic fills up his spirit.

✳

It begins around 5:00 p.m. and lasts until the sun goes down. Locals leave their homes, grocers leave their counters, and old men bring their foldout chairs to take part in the ritual. Older ladies don their finest dresses, their shiniest shoes, and their antique brooches, while teenage girls wear their pretty skirts hoping to attract the boys. Out come parents with their toddlers in strollers, their little ones on tricycles, and their dogs on leashes. As the workday ends, *la passeggiata* begins—all the townsfolk coming out for a stroll.

This evening ritual occurs in almost every Italian town—young and old slowly walking along the village's main street or square, greeting friends, sharing gossip, and conversing about the day's affairs. Once the street has been walked to the end, one turns around and begins again. With its gentle rhythm of unhurried sociability, *la passeggiata* is a tender end to the day.

We observe this sweet tradition while sitting in the main piazza of Montalcino in Tuscany, where the town's serenity is doing for Merryn what the Vatican's artworks had done for me. We'd always been different that way. When faced with stress, I'd hunger for beauty while Merryn would long for a book, a couch, and some peace. This little village is just what she needs—a place of gentle tranquility.

Perched on a hill as if in a fantasy novel, Montalcino is as quaint as it is old. Green shuttered windows punctuate thick stone walls, and flower boxes explode with fiery-red geraniums. Cobblestone paths squeeze between tall terrace houses of blue, yellow, and terracotta hues. Steep, twisting lanes lead to panoramic views of the surrounding valleys with their silvery olive orchards, vineyards, and fields. Hilltop castles, medieval abbeys, and bell towers add to Montalcino's charming feel.

But it's the village's serene soul that is proving most curative—where the only sounds are soft bird calls, solitary footsteps, and the occasional three-wheeled scooter truck whizzing produce through the street. Even in the hubbub of *la passeggiata*, where demonstrative Italian expression is plentiful, the place lacks angst or tension. As we sit at an outdoor café table, we feel heavy with rest, as if our bodies were merging with our seats.

Two ladies with neatly coiffed hair greet a third handbag-holding friend and start chatting, perhaps about the weather, perhaps about grandchildren.

"Life was so busy in Sydney," Merryn says as she watches them.

She's right. From the day we'd arrived in Sydney, our diaries had been full: me launching *Open House* and managing its expansion; directing a national radio campaign, which had me traveling to the developing world, plus taking various speaking engagements and writing projects; Merryn straddling both work and study for some years while enduring long commutes in a city notorious for its traffic congestion and delayed busses.

"I don't want us to get that busy again," she says.

A young couple stop as an older gent in a panama hat puts his newspaper under his arm and stoops to greet their little girl.

Most of the time I'd found that fast-paced Sydney life exciting. I was doing meaningful things and meeting fascinating people in rapid-fire succession. But exhaustion was a frequent reality, and after a busy weekend of speaking and broadcasting, Monday morning migraines were common. Our many IVF clinic visits had weighed like a blanket on top of this busyness, as had the stresses related to adoption. Only now do we feel the extent to which our emotional tanks had run dry. Now—as we rest, as we breathe, as we simply sit and *be*.

"Shall we?" Merryn says, nodding toward the procession.

Merryn's parents have joined us for part of our trip, and we

---

have time before we meet them for dinner. So we leave our seats and join *la passeggiata.*

Slowly we walk down the Piazza del Popolo, past the town hall and bell tower, past the shoe shop and wine shop. Slowly we stroll past the pharmacy and perfumery, past the *pasticceria* with its confectionary, past the Il Grappolo and other restaurants. Slowly we saunter past pizzerias and gelatarias as their owners stand in doorways trading salutations with their regulars.

We turn to the right and amble along Montalcino's picturesque backstreets, where rose bushes become artworks against grey and tan stone walls, and clotheslines full of fluttering towels hint at a beauty hidden in domesticity. A man rests on a park bench. A woman tends her flower bed. A couple peruse a notice board announcing engagements, births, and deaths.

Montalcino hasn't always been this place of peace. Throughout the Middle Ages it was at war with the Siennese, and an agricultural crisis in the 1950s brought the region to its knees. The town's fortunes only changed when its altitude and climate made it perfect for growing Sangiovese grapes, leading to the creation of the now famous Brunello di Montalcino wine. In its own way, Montalcino experienced resurrection.

On we stroll, down this lane and that, when we come across a wall sprayed with graffiti. "No Regrets" it says in orange and green paint.

No regrets.

After a decision as large as ours, one can wonder if the choice has been right. But as we stroll toward the Il Grappolo, sit down at our table, raise glasses of Brunello, and share a toast to all that lies ahead, there is a sense that better times are in store. We are peaceful. We are calm. We are at rest.

No regrets.

*

"This feels wrong," she says.

"Aren't we supposed to be going the other way?" I say.

We had double-read the signs and triple-checked with an attendant, but as the waterbus pulls away from the quay, it's clear we're on the wrong boat. Expecting a scenic trip down the Grand Canal of the city fêted by so many painters and poets, we instead head out toward Venice's shipping ports.

"Well, who knows what unexpected wonders we'll see going this way," I say, trying an optimistic take on the situation.

But instead of gondolas, bridges, and Baroque-style hotels, we soon see trading docks, forklifts, and overseas shipping containers.

"Oh, what wonders," Merryn says with a sarcastic smile.

It may not be the grandest start to our visit of Italy's floating metropolis, but we are still excited to be in the place where boats replace cars, waterbuses replace taxis, and gondolas fill the narrow canals that lace across the city. To our relief, we end up at the San Marco Piazza on the other side of town. We step off the boat and into a crowd of thousands swarming around the square before joining the long queue for one of the city's main attractions—the Doge's Palace.

With its paintings, sculptures, and lavishly furnished rooms, the Palace reflects the opulence of old Venetian royalty. This is epitomized by the Chamber of the Great Council, a colossal room adorned with portraits of the Doges, a ceiling full of paintings in gold-carved frames, and the largest canvas in the world—Tintoretto's "Il Paradiso"—decorating the main wall. I gaze at the ceiling while Merryn wanders through the nearby halls. I find her again in an adjacent room.

"Look at this," she says as I walk over.

Again, as at the Vatican, a room full of maps has captured Merryn's attention. She stands before one of them puzzled.

"It's supposed to be America," she says, "but look where California is."

The only US state named on the ancient map has been transplanted to the East Coast. The southern states, depicted as one large mountainous region, have "Terra Incognite" emblazoned across them. Judging by its strange shape, much of the country is "unknown land" to the artist.

"Why is China on the right?" I say, referring to another identifiable name in the painting. "And does that say 'Java' at the top?"

And then we realize why we're so disoriented. The map looks wrong not so much because it is incorrect, but because it is upside down. Those "southern states" are actually Canada.

"There's got to be a metaphor about life in that," Merryn jokes.

We step back into the piazza, ready for lunch. The crowds are dense, the cafés are expensive, a hefty fee is charged for the toilets, and there are almost no public chairs. We buy focaccia from a pizzeria and sit on the doorway step for a rest, then plan our next excursion.

Our next few hours are spent roaming the passageways that zigzag throughout the city. As in Rome, our tourist map is not to scale. Our many wrong turns are further explained when we discover that, while our map is written in Italian, Venice's signs are in Venetian. But unexpected wonders can be found when you go in a different direction.

Venice is hailed as a city of romance, and in many ways it is. Standing on one of the many footbridges that span the canals, Merryn and I watch a string of stripe-shirted gondoliers navigate their boats through the narrow channel. A young couple snuggles tight as they softly glide beneath the bridge while an accordionist plays them a tune.

Venice is also hailed as a place of beauty, and this, too, is true. Reflections of flowers and towers shimmer in its waters, and the gold domes, tessellated floors, and detailed mosaics of Saint Mark's Basilica could even rival the Vatican's splendor.

But with ticket sellers never far away, those gondola tours can resemble theme park rides rather than anything akin to romance, and Venice's billboards and tourist shops are far from most notions of beauty. The real elegance of the city lies elsewhere.

Venice's glory lies in its decay.

Those detours down the backstreets have revealed some interesting sights, like the building to our right. Its canary-yellow walls are streaked with stains from the rusty hinges of its window shutters. Chunks of stucco have broken away, exposing patches of red bricks and mortar. White sills frame dark green shutters with flaking paint. With red and yellow posies in the window boxes, the cumulative effect is delightful.

The pattern repeats as we cross another bridge; it is only the colors that change. A pink-walled building with blue, peeling shutters. A light tan facade with a faded red door. Crumbling stucco revealing red brick features. Old iron balconies on skewed upper floors.

Very few walls in Venice align. Buildings lean, tilt and bulge. Look up from those walls and you see ad-hoc additions, like a tree house built by kids who wanted more and more levels. But without its slanting lampposts and period lanterns, and its bronze-domed halls that have gone green in the rain; without its dented row boats bobbing in back-alley canals and its old pipes, wires and doorbell buttons, Venice wouldn't be the same.

The city of water, the city of wonder, the city of masks, the city of canals—Venice has been given many titles. But with its rough edges and faded paint, for me it is the city of broken beauty. In an unbalanced world where things don't square up, where dreams and realities can fail to align; in a world that so often turns upside down, where the future is uncertain and we walk in confusion, Venice is a reminder that light can still shine—that beauty can emerge through the cracks.

"If we're not going to have a family," I say as we ride the train back to our hotel that evening, "let's make the most of the life we have."

"Let's be the best aunty and uncle we can be to our nephews and nieces," Merryn says.

———

"Let's be there for our friends' kids if they ever need to talk," I say.

I think of the many single people who have used the opportunities inherent in their situation to live vibrant, productive lives—like the Bible scholar John Stott who used his singleness to write books, serve his church, and teach around the world. As a childless couple, we have similar resources of mobility, flexibility, and time.

"The truth is," I say, "we won't have the financial pressures that would've come with children. We can do things we couldn't have done with little mouths to feed."

"Like taking some time to write your books," Merryn says.

"We have the flexibility to travel," I add, "without needing to think about schooling."

"Maybe I could get some short-term international postings," she says.

"I could record interviews as we go," I say. "Between writing books, I could start an international radio show."

"Is that before or after the TV program?"

"Before, but after the world speaking tour."

We laugh, then fall quiet for a while, watching the world rush by the window as the last rays of dusk soften. No opportunity, whether real or imagined, makes up for not having a child. But it has been good to realize that we have possibilities.

Merryn leans into my shoulder. She says, "Let's live an adventure."

And I can't help but wonder—

—wonder whether the joyful play of those bubble-chasing

children and the grand designs of Rome's wonders; whether the beauty of the Vatican's galleries and those tranquil strolls along Montalcino's laneways haven't begun to revive us.

And I can't help but wonder if there's room to hope—

—to hope that some beauty can spring from our own brokenness, as the stained colors of Venice's walls redeem that crumbling city.

And I can't help but wonder—

—wonder if one day God's frustrating silence might even start to make sense.

5

Wrestling with God
on the Mountain

June 2, 2011

Our little red train winds its way through the vales and gorges of the countryside. Snow-capped mountains tower high above us, the mist wafting from their peaks to become wispy white clouds on a cyan sky. The hills are adorned with masses of fern trees, like thick velvety stubble, and the sheer slopes descend to valleys of yellow daisies full of wandering goats, singing birds, and grazing cows with clanging cowbells. We pass small, secluded villages made of little chalets, where handmade shingles dangle from little grocery stores. There are little yellow pubs with pretty shuttered windows, and little blue hotels with softly puffing chimneys. There are little white churches perched on rocky precipices, with steeples and bells and old stone walls. There are castles and waterfalls and gently-flowing streams, and old trucks negotiating hairpin bends on winding, narrow roads.

Farther on our little red train goes, snaking between the majestic Swiss Alps, until we arrive at the small town of Aigle. There we board a bus and ride some of those hairpin bends up the mountain, through the velvety stubble, around the hills and fields, alighting at the Alpine village of Huémoz. We drag our suitcases up a stony path to a large three-story chalet, step into an annexed entrance piled with shoes, and knock on the front door.

A man holding a broom opens it to us.

"Hi there," he says. "Welcome to L'Abri."

*

L'Abri defies neat descriptions. Calling it a retreat center implies luxury, as if it were all spas, saunas, and massage tables. Calling it a study center sounds too cerebral, as if it were all courses, classes, and seminar papers. Calling it a commune is even worse, conjuring up images of dreadlocks, peace pipes, and flowers in navels. While one does come to L'Abri to retreat, study, and live in community, there are no cross-legged gurus or shiny seminar rooms. And there are certainly no spas or masseurs.

Established by Francis and Edith Schaeffer in the 1950s as a safe place to think through life and faith, L'Abri (French for "the Shelter") started when a few university students began visiting the Schaeffer's home to talk about philosophy and Christianity. Word soon spread about the Schaeffer's hospitality, and truth seekers from around the world began trekking up the mountain. Today, L'Abri centers operate in numerous countries.

"You must be Sheridan and Merryn," says a warm-faced woman coming down the stairs. "I'm Kay. Let me show you around."

Kay turns out to be one of L'Abri's workers, a house mother of sorts, whose inviting smile, Texan accent, and sharp wit we quickly grow to like. We follow her around the large house, named Chalet Bellevue, which we discover is the central hub in a small cluster of chalets making up L'Abri.

"We call this the Rembrandt Room," Kay says with a smile as we look through the first door off the foyer into a cozy nook filled with art and poetry books, with a reading chair, footstool, and balcony. "We have most of our meals here," Kay adds as we walk on into a large dining room with big windows, burgundy walls, and wooden tables and chairs. "And through here is the common room," she says as we head into a large space full of old couches covered with throw rugs, waist-level shelves filled with books, worn sideboards holding potted plants, and a piano in the corner. While the floorboards are worn and the coffee tables are scratched, the place doesn't feel rundown but comfy.

We descend some stairs to a basement area where Kay flicks a switch that illuminates a long corridor. "There are baskets in each bathroom for your laundry," she says, "and here's where you collect it once it's washed." She opens the doors of an old closet to reveal shelves of neatly piled shirts, shorts, jeans, sweaters, socks, bras, and underwear.

———

"So, we just rummage through the underwear to find our own?" Merryn says.

"Yes, of course," Kay answers. "Communal living at its best, huh?"

"Uh-huh," we say.

"You know that days at L'Abri are broken into three sections, don't you?" Kay says as we head back up to the foyer. "After breakfast you'll be rostered to either study or do chores around the property. The chores keep the costs down and are part of living as a community. After lunch you'll do the opposite of what you did in the morning—either chores or study—and after dinner it's free time. You'll also be asked to wash up after one meal each day. Now, let's get you to your room."

We carry our suitcases up the creaky wooden stairs to the second level. A series of dorm rooms open off the left side of the hallway, while bathrooms and toilets are on the right.

"And you know about the shower rations?" Kay says, looking me in the eye.

"No more than three showers per week," I say.

"No more than *two* showers per week," she says. "As you may know, Switzerland is a very expensive place to live. Our hot water bills are astronomical."

"What if Sheridan and I shared a bath?" Merryn says.

"Sounds good to me," I say, delighted at Merryn's newfound adventurousness. It must be the invigorating Swiss air.

"I mean shared the bath *water*," she clarifies. "Couldn't we then have four baths a week instead?

"Well, I guess so," says Kay, chuckling.

"Phew," Merryn says.

"How long have you been married?"

"Fifteen years this December."

"Well, the dorms are all four-to-a-room," Kay says, striking immediate horror into both of us. "But you'll be glad to know we've put you in a room by yourselves. It's just over here." She walks to the first door in the hallway. It opens into a small corner room with a wardrobe and a chest of drawers.

And two single bunk beds.

"We call it the Honeymoon Suite," Kay says, laughing loudly before leaving us to unpack.

Our room has, shall we say, personality. There are two nails on the back of the door to hang our towels on, and a second latch has been added to make the door close properly. The bunks are handmade from untreated pine, and a previous guest has left a packet of chewing gum on the wardrobe shelf. But when we open our curtains, those snow-capped Swiss Alps fill our cottage windows like art in a picture frame.

We wheel in our suitcases, put our clothes in the drawers, take another look out our windows, then sit on the thin mattress of the bottom bunk.

Silence.

All we hear is pure, peaceful silence.

There's a knock at the door. "Hi, I'm Jasmine," says a twenty-something girl with a Canadian accent. "Kay asked me to take you down to see the library. By the way, if either of you want an extra shower, I'll trade one of mine for some chocolate."

And we know then that our stay at L'Abri is going to be memorable.

August 2010

"I particularly feel we should pray for you, Merryn," the young woman says.

"Yes, I sense that too," says another present.

The woman walks around the couch and lays her hands on Merryn's shoulders. "You have a broken heart," she says, "and that has disrupted your relationship with God."

Merryn nods and a tear rolls down her cheek.

"I don't know what this means," the woman continues, "but I feel we should pray for new life to be birthed within you."

A lounge room in suburban Sydney and another prayer meeting—this one called by Louise, the wife of our pastor, who has watched us sink lower and lower after successive IVF attempts. She has gathered a small group of church members sensitive to God's voice to minister to us. In an effort to guard against personal feelings being misunderstood for divine guidance, the group hasn't been told about our infertility. The first half of the night is given to them praying and sharing what they sense God might be saying to us; our actual problem is revealed later.

The evening proceeds in an intriguing way in light of this purposed ignorance. While prayers are prayed for me, it is Merryn who is focused on. A broken heart. Disrupted relationship with God. New life to be "birthed" from within. The words seem apt for her. When we share our infertility story, someone says that an image of a womb has been on her mind during the prayer time.

"Is it healing that you're seeking from God?" someone asks.

"We've had prayer for healing many times before," I say, "and we're certainly open for more. But what we most need now is guidance."

"Over these last few years," Merryn says, "we have prayed through every option of having a family—whether we should adopt, foster, do IVF, wait for healing, or remain childless. And we've never had a clear answer."

"Although it would be hard," I add, "it would even be a mercy to hear God say no—that we are not to have a child. At least we could grieve and move on."

"Our real prayer request now," Merryn says, "is to know whether we should continue with IVF or stop."

We settle back into our seats, bow our heads, begin to seek God, and wait. With the first half of the night so encouraging, we wait in expectancy.

Silence.

Patiently we wait, like the widow in Jesus' story, who is promised that her needs will be met if she's persistent. We wait for a word, a sense, a whisper, a leading. We wait for God's voice. We wait for his prompting.

Five minutes pass. Then ten. Then fifteen.

Silence.

All we hear is awkward, empty silence.

No answers are given tonight—as has been the case for the past decade. Our praying saints are baffled at the evening's change of tone and, even with the earlier encouragement, we feel a little like orphans: Left by God to fend for ourselves. Left to struggle on alone.

September 2010

Merryn writes in her journal:

Almost more difficult than the infertility, has been the constant silence of God. It's plain courtesy to answer someone's e-mail. We've been sending them to God for ten years and getting no reply.

October 2010

I wish I could trust God again, I wish I could trust that there's some grand plan or reason behind God not giving us a child.

December 2010

Or maybe God is just mean.

June 3, 2011

"So, those are the questions you've brought with you," she says, gently rocking on her easy chair: "Why God has been silent to you, and whether there's a reason for what you've been through."

"And whether God is a meanie," Merryn adds, only half in jest.

Merryn sits with Karryn, another L'Abri worker, in her small chalet just down the hill from Chalet Bellevue. Karryn's black-and-white Border Collie has rested its head on Merryn's leg and is enjoying having its silky fur stroked. With a friendly dog, a cozy home, the warm morning light, and Karryn's readiness to listen, Merryn shares a little of our wilderness journey and the questions it has raised.

While there are weekly lectures on various topics, there is no set curriculum at L'Abri. The beauty of the place is that you come with your own questions and are given space and a tutor to help find answers.

"Basically," Merryn says, "I need to work God out."

"And how long are you here for?" Karryn asks.

"Two weeks."

"Well, good luck with that one," she says, as they both laugh at the task and the timeframe. "But here are some books that you might find helpful."

*

There are no billboards here in Huémoz, or flashing neon signs. There are no TVs at L'Abri, or radios allowed in rooms. You hand in your laptop on arrival, getting it back only on your days off. And all of this is intentional. Take away these distractions, remove all the noise and interruptions, and you're left with beauty and people and conversation and God.

We've needed this — space for undistracted contemplation.

*

"Well, don't you look a treat," she says.

I've returned to our room following an afternoon of clipping, weeding, and shoveling. I'm sweaty, my jeans are dirty, there are scratches on my arms, and my feet smell. Merryn winces as I flop down next to her on the bottom bunk.

"I'm exhausted," I say. "How has your day been?"

"Good," she says, though she's clearly concerned at my effect on the duvet. "I helped in the kitchen this morning, then studied this afternoon. No, please don't take your socks off."

"What did you read?" I say, pulling my sock back up.

"Philip Yancey's book *Disappointment with God.*"

I heave myself deeper onto the bed and swivel round to face her, signaling my readiness to listen if she's wanting to talk.

"Yancey makes some good points," she says thoughtfully. "He says that people often have faith until something bad happens, then they get disappointed with God. This can then lead to doubt and, often, feelings of anger or betrayal. That resonated with me. It was nice to know I wasn't alone with such feelings."

I nod.

"Yancey uses the example of his friend Richard, who lost his faith after a bunch of bad experiences. Richard had three questions about God through his ordeal: is God unfair, is God silent, and is God hidden? Richard's idea was that if only God would reveal himself, speak clearly, and treat people as they deserve, then he could believe. But since he felt God had been hidden, silent, and unfair to him, he couldn't believe anymore.

"But Yancey goes on to say," Merryn continues, "that God

treated the Israelites just the way Richard wanted, during the Exodus. He was visible to them . . ."

"In the pillar of cloud and fire," I say, following along.

"And he spoke clearly to them . . ."

"On Mount Sinai, through Moses," I add.

"And he treated people fairly through the covenant, with the consequences of breaking it clearly spelled out and agreed to by them beforehand. God was visible, he spoke and he was fair, but the result wasn't the Israelite's faith but their disobedience."

"Like the golden calf episode."

"And," Merryn says, "even with all of this, the Israelites didn't feel close to God either. In fact, they said, 'Let us not hear the voice of the Lord our God or see this great fire anymore, or we will die.'"

"So," I say, "if God always spoke to us clearly, there's no guarantee we'd have any more faith or any better relationship with him."

"That's what Yancey's getting at," she says. "And when God *is* silent, which he often is in the Bible—think of David in the Psalms rousing on God for hiding his face—Yancey says we shouldn't interpret it as a lack of care or concern. That's what Job thought and God corrected him about it."

Thank you, God, I whisper silently. Merryn's spiritual life has withered in the heat of our wilderness journey, and these words feel like green shoots springing through the dust.

"Still," she says, "that doesn't explain why he didn't heal us when he could have."

"It's a good thing we've got another few days here, huh?" I say, putting my hand on her knee.

"Maybe all my questions will be answered in just two weeks," she says, smiling, "and I'll never have a doubt about God again."

"Hey, I've got a question for you," I say.

"What?"

"Do we have any chocolate? I'm thinking of taking Jasmine up on her offer."

"Sorry," she says. "But there's always that stick of gum in the wardrobe. Maybe she'll swap that for a shower."

"I'll go and see—but not before giving you a kiss!"

I lunge playfully onto Merryn, rubbing my sweaty face all over her cheek. She falls back onto the pillow, squealing and giggling.

"What are you two doing?" says a female voice, seemingly from nowhere.

It's a student leaning out from the front balcony, peering into our window. She has a giant grin on her face. Merryn screams and rips the curtain closed, making us look like the guiltiest innocent couple ever to have lodged in the Honeymoon Suite.

✱

"Do believers ever consider that the 'answers' they get to prayer might simply be their own expectations fulfilled?" The question came during lunch today. That's what I like about this place: the table is open to all, irrespective of faith or philosophy, and many come unconvinced about God and Christianity.

The opposite of faith isn't doubt but indifference,

because those who doubt are still engaged with the question while the indifferent don't care. People here aren't indifferent; they just need a safe place to explore their doubts.

*

"I'm starting to wonder if I've gotten God all wrong," she says.

An evening stroll down the hillside paths of Huémoz. Rays of afternoon light break through the drifting clouds to progressively illuminate each village in the valley. The magnificent Mont Blanc glows in the distance; one almost expects Moses to appear, clutching his stone tablets, his face radiant. But Merryn walks in the shadows.

"I've always thought everything happened for a reason," she says, "but now I'm not so sure."

I put my arm around her as we walk.

"I've been reading a book today," she says, "by a theologian named Greg Boyd. Have you heard of him?"

"I've read some of his work, yes," I say.

"Well, this book is called *Is God to Blame?*[1] Boyd is also a pastor, and he tells the story of a woman named Melanie who came to see him because she wanted to have a passionate relationship with God, which she'd previously had but lost. She was also depressed and things weren't good with her husband. It turned out Melanie had married later in life and tried to start a family straight away. She was told she wouldn't be able to conceive because of a medical condition. Then, miraculously, she did conceive. But during birth the umbilical cord wrapped around the baby's neck and strangled it to death. It had been a perfectly healthy child. Melanie and her husband were never able to conceive again."

I feel sick as Merryn tells the story.

"Melanie went to her pastor, who told her that everything happens for a reason and that God probably wanted to teach her something through the experience."

I wince.

"It's an extreme case," Merryn says, "but isn't that what we usually tell people who suffer? That God must have allowed the suffering for a reason—for some greater good? Many people have said that to us about not having children."

"That's true," I say.

"Boyd says this whole idea is wrong," Merryn continues, "because it stems from the belief that all suffering in the world is part of God's will—either because he has preordained it, in the Calvinist sense, or because he has allowed it. Yet it's hard to love a God who allowed your baby to be strangled."

"And even harder to love a God who prearranged it to happen," I add.

"But if everything that happens is God's will, either because it's been preordained or allowed," Merryn says, "then why did Jesus heal the sick and cast out demons? Doesn't this show that sickness and suffering is *not* God's will? If God's will is done, why did Jesus come at all? Doesn't it make more sense to say that God's will *isn't* being done in the world and Jesus came to change that?"

"I don't know of any Christian who would say that suffering is God's ultimate will," I say. "Heaven is the place where God's will is completely achieved, and it's clear from Scripture there's no suffering there. But I see the incongruity: if we say that all suffering on earth is either preordained or allowed by God, why is God, throughout the Scriptures, so intent on eradicating sin and evil and the suffering it brings?"

"And why should we even pray?" Merryn adds. "If God has already preordained or allowed the suffering to happen, what good is it asking him to change things? Unless you believe that God changes his mind in response to prayer."

"Which many people don't," I say, "because we believe God already knows the best thing to do and doesn't need our suggestions."

"Exactly. So God decided that we wouldn't have a family, and all our prayers and the IVF rounds and the adoption program was never going to change that," she says, tears starting to well in her eyes.

We continue down the narrow pathway, passing dark wood chalets with neatly stacked log piles and old barns full of farm tools and hay bales before turning into the open field.

"According to Boyd," Merryn says, resuming her train of thought, "everything *doesn't* happen for a reason because God's will isn't always achieved."

"How does he reason that?" I ask.

"If I understand him correctly," she says, "Boyd explains it this way: First, God gave humans free will, and by doing so took the risk that we'd use that freedom to do evil rather than good.

God won't revoke our free will, even when we do evil. And that means that our wills, not just his, operate in the world, whether for good or ill."

"So the Holocaust, for example, was Hitler's will, not God's," I add.

"Right. The second reason is that there are other forces in the world—demonic forces—that also have free will. We don't know how much these spirits affect what happens in the world, but why would the apostle Paul teach the Ephesians to put on the 'full armor of God' and battle these 'principalities and powers' if they didn't have real influence in our lives?"

"That's a good point," I say, "but is Boyd suggesting that God doesn't interfere in their free will either?"

"I think that's what he's saying. God doesn't revoke the free will of his creatures, which is why they have real influence and why there's evil and suffering."

"What does he say about the way God *does* intervene in the world?"

"According to Boyd," she says, "God does sometimes intervene supernaturally in history and individual lives. But there are two reasons why he often doesn't: One, again, is our free will. Since God won't revoke our freedom, he has to accept what we do. The other is the laws of nature. God created the world in such a way that tampering with its laws will bring chaos. He gives the example of two people in the same place, praying—one for rain and the other for clear skies. God can't make both happen at the same time without radically altering the nature of the universe and causing massive ramifications as a result."

"I get that," I say. "The flip side, though, is that it suggests God isn't in complete control of the world."

"Boyd says there are some things God can't do, not because God isn't powerful enough to do them, but because he limits himself to the constraints of the universe he's created."

"That idea isn't new," I say. "Harold Kushner popularized it some years ago in *When Bad Things Happen to Good People*. But we know that miraculous answers to prayer do happen, where the laws of nature are interrupted. Remember that interview I did with Sean George last year?"

"The doctor in Western Australia?"

"He was dead for fifty-five minutes, as all the medical equipment proved. Then his wife walked into the room, took his hand, prayed a simple prayer, and his heart started to beat again.[2] Boyd agrees that God sometimes intervenes supernaturally; does he say what determines when God will, won't, or can't intervene?"

"He says there are a number of factors determining whether our prayer is granted or not," she says. "God's will is one of them, but also human free will, angelic and demonic free will, the faith of the person praying and the person being prayed for, the number of people praying, how persistent the prayer is, the number and strength of spirits battling in the unseen world, and the presence of sin, among others."

By now we've followed our path down the hill and back up again, looping round to return to a small fountain near the village church. We take a sip of the trickling mountain water, then rest against the wall of the stone trough.

———

"Could it be true?" Merryn says, looking at me. "Could God have nothing to do with our childlessness? Could we have attributed our infertility to God's will when it's actually come from Satan or demons? Instead of it being part of God's 'grand plan' for us, could the genetic problems in your sperm DNA stem from some human cause, maybe even generations back? I don't know—maybe a bad diet or poor medical treatment, or living in a polluted area or something? I think my feelings for God have cooled over these last ten years because I've thought all this was his doing. But maybe God couldn't do anything about it. Maybe he is just as upset about us not having children as I am."

I put my arm around her again.

"It's all very confusing," she says. "And disconcerting. After all these years as a Christian, could I really have gotten God so wrong?"

*

"Tell me what you think," she says as we rest by the fountain.

I look out across the valley, trying to collect my thoughts into something whole. But as soon as those thoughts gather, another counterpoint or verse of Scripture comes to mind and they scatter again, like a gardener raking leaves in the breeze. Theologians have raked these same leaves for centuries, gathering them into different shaped piles. Few have successfully held all the leaves together, and none of the piles have been neat. The problem of God and suffering isn't easily solved.

"There's a lot to agree with in what you've said," I say, after a long pause. "I do believe we are free to act in both good and evil ways, making us and not God responsible for our actions. I do believe prayer changes history, not just our attitude to what happens: Elijah prayed and Israel's drought broke; the early church prayed and Peter miraculously escaped prison. Scripture is full of commands to pray, promising that it effects change. And I do believe Boyd is right that spiritual warfare is real and must be fought."

"I don't think I've taken that seriously enough," Merryn says.

"I've neglected it too," I say. "I also think Boyd is on to something with that rain and sunshine analogy. We tend to think that our prayer request will only affect us, when, actually, we're part of a complex, interrelated world, and God granting us what we want could significantly affect others, even later in history. There must be so many factors we don't see."

"Yancey makes a similar point in his book," Merryn adds. "Job knew nothing about the drama that was going on in heaven when he lost his health, his children, and his possessions. Our human viewpoints are limited."

"I think that's very true."

"But if God allows human beings and demons to have free will," she says, "how much is he really in control of the world?"

"Maybe more than Boyd believes," I say tentatively.

Merryn waits for my explanation.

"I haven't read his book," I say, "so I may have this wrong, but from what you've said of Boyd's theology, the picture I get is of God running the universe like a house that he built but then locked himself out of. Occasionally he can reach in through an open window and intervene, but otherwise he has little control over what happens inside, with humans and spirits doing what they like in there. I just don't think that's true.

"Joseph could say that while his brothers had planned evil by selling him into slavery, God had meant it for good. Satan had to get God's permission to oppress Job. In these two stories alone, both human free will and demonic free will operate within God's will, not outside of it. Jesus said not even a sparrow falls to the ground outside of God's will."

"So, you believe it is actually God's will that we don't have children?" Merryn says.

"Not his perfect will but his permissive will," I say. "For the time being, in this fallen, broken world, he permits things that he hates."

"Why?"

"Well," I say sheepishly, "to achieve some greater good." I recoil inside as I say the words, knowing I've spiraled back to an answer Merryn already finds unsatisfactory.

"And what greater good could come from a baby being strangled at birth?" she says quietly.

"I have no idea," I say with a sigh, as the breeze rustles my neat pile of leaves.

*

"Ready?" Merryn says, popping her head through the kitchen door.

Both of us have study sessions rostered this morning, and

after I finish my breakfast wash-up duties, we slip on our shoes and take the stone path down to L'Abri's library. With one wall full of books and the other full of windows overlooking the valley, the library's downstairs room is bright and cozy. The Alpine air is brisk this morning, and Merryn makes us mugs of hot coffee. We've brought good quantities of Swiss chocolate with us, and with blankets on our laps and books on our desks, we are soon ready for a morning of study. But something is bothering me.

"Our conversation last night," I say to Merryn as she opens up *Is God to Blame?* "—something about it has left me troubled."

"What is it?" she says, turning to me.

"Well, if what Greg Boyd says is true," I say, "then I can't help feeling that we failed."

Merryn furrows her brow.

"If God did want us to have a child," I say, "then it follows, from Boyd's account of things, that we lost the battle to have one. Either we didn't pray enough or with enough faith, didn't have enough people praying for us, or didn't engage in enough spiritual warfare. The demons outnumbered the angels. We failed. Satan won."

"I guess that could be one interpretation," Merryn says dejectedly.

"When I think of all the prayers we and others prayed over the years about this," I say, "that is a less than comforting thought. What more could we have done? We prayed until we were exhausted."

Merryn turns and stares reflectively out the window for a while, then picks up her book and continues reading.

———

*

"We keep wondering why God hasn't intervened in our situation," I say. "But sometimes I wonder if he has."

Some days have passed since Merryn and I last discussed the problem of God and suffering. Merryn has needed space to process her reading, the topic still prone to bringing tears. I raise it again cautiously as we wander through a field of white and yellow daisies, walking up the mountain to the nearby town of Villars on our afternoon off.

"How do you mean?" Merryn says.

"I had this lady call in while I was on-air one night," I explain. "She was the mother of a severely autistic child who needed round-the-clock care. Her marriage had failed due to the stress of the situation. She hadn't had a full night's sleep in years, or a holiday, because government-funded respite was in short supply and she couldn't afford private care. It was clear this woman was dedicated to her son, and yet she said, 'If I'm honest, knowing how his life and our lives have turned out, I sometimes wish he had never been born.' I've always wondered if we'd have been able to cope in her situation."

"You mean, if we'd have had a severely disabled child?" Merryn says.

"The possibility was always there in my mind, especially given the CF thing."

In the course of doing IVF, a test had revealed that I carried the cystic fibrosis gene. Many people carry this gene, in fact, and the only real risk comes when starting a family with another carrier. Merryn was tested and found clear but, along-side the other DNA problems with my sperm, it was obvious we were always working with shaky genetic material.

"If God intervened to stop something bad from happening," Merryn says, "why didn't he go further and make something good happen instead?"

"I don't know," I say. "But it seems to me that we yell at God when bad things happen, and we yell at God when good things don't happen. We never think that God may have prevented some-thing bad from happening that we never knew about, or withheld a seemingly good thing because it was actually bad for us."

"Maybe," she says in a less-than-convinced tone.

We follow our dirt path out of the sunlit field and into the forest, where we wind our way in the shadows toward Villars.

"I don't fully understand it all, love," I say. "But I'm still hold-ing out that God is doing something in all this—that there *is* a reason for our infertility. There was a reason why God didn't remove Paul's 'thorn in the flesh,' and even Jesus didn't have all his prayers answered—remember Gethsemane? Maybe God has some redemptive purpose for our pain too."

"Maybe," she says.

*

If there is a reason for our childlessness, will we ever know it? When God broke his silence to Job, he told him nothing about the cause or purpose of his suffering. God simply displayed himself as the all-powerful, all-knowing, majestic Creator of the world who is intimately involved in its working. And that was enough for Job. "My ears had heard of you, but now my eyes have seen you."

God rewarded Job but never answered his questions. Job encountered God and no longer needed answers.

*

Cutlery clinks, candles flicker, and laughter fills the room. There are songs and cheers and lots of applause, and a table full of homemade food—chili and rice and handmade tortillas; pasta, cornbread, and two flavors of soup. Someone else tries their hand at some L'Abri-style amusement as the coffee comes out and dessert is served.

Dinners at Chalet Bellevue are rarely dull. With an array of personalities from so many nations, there is always a story to hear or a joke to tell. But tonight a few students have made an extra effort, pulling out the candles and tablecloths and arranging some entertainment. A hipster girl with slimline glasses plays a tune on a purple ukulele. Another performs a violin piece, while a third cuts a funky bass riff on her cello. Shower-swapper Jasmine pulls out her guitar to sing a song for a soon-departing friend, saying how *little* she'll miss her because she *never* really liked her—her sarcasm soon mixed with tears. Bonds formed at L'Abri often last for years.

When the festivities end, I join others in the common room while Merryn heads to the student computer tucked just behind the Rembrandt Room. There she logs into her e-mail account and types a letter bound for a pastor's wife in Sydney.

Hi Louise,

Well, the time has come. We leave L'Abri tomorrow after a really valuable stay. The mountains around us are spectacular, we've met some wonderful people, and we've had time to read and reflect and pray. We're glad we came.

As you know, I wanted to resolve some specific questions while I was here: why God remained silent to us, whether "everything happens for a reason," and how good God really is. Over the past two weeks these questions have opened up others, like whether God is truly powerful, how much he controls life's events, and even whether he knows the future or not (let's have a chat about open theism one day). It's all been rather intense. I spent much of today reading a novel for some relief.

If nothing else, these two weeks have reminded me how important theology is. My spiritual life has shriveled over the last ten years, possibly because I've held incorrect beliefs about God. I don't think I even realized the beliefs I held; it's been eye-opening to have them revealed through all this reading. But, gosh, some of these theologians need to write in a more accessible style. When they write in abstractions, they talk only among themselves, not to those of us *needing* answers. At times it felt like the most readable books had the least biblical arguments while those with more promise were impossible to understand.

Have I found answers to my questions? Not yet, not for all of them. I do see now that there are many complexities involved in God answering our prayers the way we want, many of which we may never understand. The world is fallen and that's affected the genes of all humans; if the result is poor eyesight for some, why not fertility problems for others? We don't blame God when we need glasses, so maybe God isn't to blame for our childlessness either. And while miracles do happen, they are rare; maybe with more of them real faith would be rarer still. But none of this explains why God didn't intervene in *our* situation. There may be a grand plan involved or there may not. I really don't know yet. In Romans 8 we're told that in all things God works for the good of those who love him. I'm holding on to that for the time being.

And so I guess that means I have made some progress. Even with so much remaining a mystery, I no longer think that God is a meanie. Maybe that was always the more important question to address.

In a couple of days we arrive in Oxford—the beginning of a new chapter in our lives. We're looking forward to getting there.

With love to you both,
Merryn

*

And as a small group of new friends wave us away, our bus pulls off from L'Abri. We drive through the village then make our descent—down the Alpine hills, around the hairpin bends, past

barns and fields and through velvety stubble, into valleys of daisies then on to Aigle station, where another little train takes us
past more streams and castles, and more churches on precipices
with old stone walls, then drops us at Geneva to take a bus and
then board a plane to fly to the UK and start a new chapter.

Sometime later, Louise in Sydney forwards us an e-mail—
sent from someone who'd been invited to that prayer meeting
in August 2010 but hadn't been able to attend. Graham had still
prayed for us, though, while being unaware of our situation.

Dear Louise,

I have no idea what the Voyseys are dealing with and
may be off the mark here, but while I've been praying for
them, I've gotten one strong and consistent impression: God
is opening a ministry opportunity for them that they should
embrace. I also sense that this opportunity will either include
time overseas or be based overseas.

I share that for what it's worth.

Graham

We take our seats on the British Airways plane at Geneva
International Airport. After two weeks wrestling with God on
the mountain, we are about to fly to our new overseas home.

To a new and unexpected career opportunity for Merryn.

And other possibilities yet to be known.

6

A Home Among the Spires

July 2011

The flowerpots along Broad Street burst with color. We rush by them on our bicycles, passing the medieval walls of Balliol College, the historic Blackwell's bookshop, and the classic Sheldonian Theatre. Turning right, we pass the Venice-inspired Bridge of Sighs that spans New College Lane and the Bodleian Library with its millions of books overflowing into underground tunnels beneath the city center. We peddle through the cobblestone square, around the iconic Radcliffe Camera building, then down the passage beside the University Church of St. Mary the Virgin, cross the High Street, and take the little lane down to the Bear Inn before turning left to ride past Christ Church Cathedral.

John Wycliffe the Bible translator, Aldous Huxley the writer, and the famed poet Gerard Manley Hopkins once walked the hallways of Balliol. Handel premiered his oratorio *Athalia* at the Sheldonian Theatre. Methodist leader John Wesley preached historic sermons at St. Mary's, and Lewis Carroll wrote *Alice in Wonderland* at Christ Church, basing his character on the Cathedral dean's daughter.

The poet John Donne attended Hertford College near the Bodleian, and T. S. Eliot studied nearby at Merton. William Penn was at Christ Church College before founding Pennsylvania, and Shakespeare used to lodge at the nearby Crown Tavern.

Oscar Wilde and George Bernard Shaw traipsed to Blackwell's to buy books, and up the road at the Eagle and Child pub, C. S. Lewis, J. R. R. Tolkien, and other members of the famous Inklings group met on Tuesdays to read each other's work.

There's a story on every corner of Oxford's main streets. Each sandstone brick of its university walls is soaked with the conversations of the greats.

We get off our bikes and walk through Christ Church meadow.

It's still hard to believe—but this meadow and those bricks are now home.

*

"How do I look?" she says.

"Like the prettiest medical statistician at Oxford University."

Merryn stands in the kitchen of the small holiday flat that serves as our temporary home until our belongings arrive from Australia. She is dressed in a new taupe shirt, charcoal slacks, black shoes, and a silver pendant that I bought her a few years back. She looks smart but not overdressed.

"You think so?" she says, smiling.

"Honey, when those bespectacled number-crunchers see you today, they'll spill their weak tea down their cardigans."

Merryn has been anxious about her first day at work—about starting off on the right foot and fitting in well. These new clothes are a confidence boost. After a couple of weeks of flurry, she'll walk into that office at least *looking* like she's ready.

Our bus from Heathrow airport had pulled into Oxford on a grey and drizzly afternoon. After a cab ride to our accommodation, we'd trudged through the rain, determined to have our first dinner in the country at a cozy English pub, and had woken the following morning to singing birds, frolicking squirrels, clear skies, and sunshine. With its small bedroom, cramped kitchen, and lounge room ceiling so low I can't stand up straight, our flat is typical of much English housing. But after buying our bicycles—the vehicle of the true Oxonian in a town of medieval streets and limited parking—it is proving a fine base to begin exploring our new land.

We've found Oxford a new experience in many delightful ways. Unlike pushy Sydney-siders, Britons politely form single-line queues at bus stops and are quick to apologize when *you* bump into *them*. You go "for a curry" for a quick meal here, rather than "for Thai" in Australia, and the best pubs have chairs that don't match, and they welcome dogs and cats inside. Brits drive on the left, walk on the right, and are unsure what to do when a cyclist comes down the path. The humor is full of irony, local libraries carry arty European films, and the radio stations play all my favorite bands.

Another delight has been the conversations we've overheard, unlike anything we would hear back home. There was the man who answered his cell phone with, "Lord *Astonbury!* How *marvelous* to hear from you." The woman walking with a colleague who said, "Well, when I did my *first* PhD in neurology . . ." And the man at the cheese counter who said to his wife, "Oooh, I could *devour* a piece of *Wensleydale*." We've found the variety of dialects fascinating too, with Cockney ("Wot you mean you ain't got nuffing wif ya?") and Oxbridge ("Do hurry up, dear. We're running *awfully* late") alongside Irish, Jamaican, European, and other accents. And we've had many a chuckle hearing the odd person sounding their *R*s as *W*s, like the TV presenter who said, "The wegency pewiod was an ewa of wampant woyal extwavagance, but misewy and distwess for the underpwivileged."

Stonehenge is only an hour's drive from Oxford, as is Stratford-upon-Avon, where Shakespeare was born. While we've been itching to hire a car and visit these locations, the past two weeks have been consumed with more menial concerns—like getting bank accounts and mobile phones and learning where to buy clothes. *Is Barclays a reputable bank?* we've wondered. Is Debenhams like Kmart in Australia, or David Jones? Is Sainsbury's best for groceries, or is Tesco or ASDA? Unfamiliar with English companies, brand names, and chain stores, we've found buying the most basic items tiring. In a new country you start again, learning new customs and bus routes and where to source things. For a while this can feel disconcerting.

But after a day visiting clothes stores, we'd found Merryn a new outfit, and she is now ready to ride her bike into town and start work.

"I hope it's a good job," she says with concern in her eyes. "We've come a long way for it not to work out."

"It will be fine," I say reassuringly, though I've feared the same thing. The last thing Merryn needs is another letdown.

"What are you going to do today?" she asks.

"Oh, you know," I say, "write a few e-mails and things."

I give Merryn a kiss, then see her to the door. I say a prayer as she rides off down the street, then I walk back to the kitchen and sit down at the table.

And wonder what my life is now to be.

*

Hi Adrian.

Well, we've made it to the UK and after a couple of weeks in Oxford are starting to get a feel for the place. I absolutely love this country, its history, and its beauty, although I realize our honeymoon feelings will be sorely challenged when our first English winter comes.

Merryn headed off to the university this morning—her first day on the job. Hoping it all goes well there. I'm not quite sure what my future holds yet. I have some media contacts to follow up with, so we'll see where they lead. In the meantime I'm going to try completing a book that I've been writing for the last couple of years. I have the time to focus on it now. I've attached a few chapters—would you mind reading them? I would value feedback from the great Adrian Plass.

I still can't believe that we're in England. Our "Resurrection Year" has begun. Thank you for giving us such a wonderful phrase at a time when we needed it most.

Sheridan Voysey

*

The latch of the front door rattles. Merryn walks in, drops her bag on the floor, takes off her shoes, then finds me in the kitchen.

"How was it?" I say, scanning her face for the answer.

"It was good," she says, smiling.

"Is that good-good or, you know, *really* good?"

"Really good."

And she gives me a hug.

*

Merryn's boss turns out to be a Christian, and they have lots in common. The job looks exciting, with opportunity for promotion. She's even been given time to work on some overseas aid projects—just what she wanted. Thank you, God. This job is a gift for Merryn.

I cycled down the Botley Road this morning. The air was misty, and the rising sun cast fingers of light across the field as it filtered through the trees—like an outstretched hand granting a blessing. After those weary years in the wilderness, perhaps Oxford is our promised land.

August 2011

I wake groggily from sleep, as if a noise has just woken me.

Ding-dong. Ding-dong.

"Is that . . . ?" Merryn says sleepily.

" . . . the doorbell," I say.

Merryn rolls over and checks her bedside clock. "Who on earth would be on our doorstep at this time of night?" she says.

I pull back the sheets, pull on my track pants, and start walking down the creaky stairs of our new rented flat. We moved in just a week ago after our furniture arrived from Sydney.

"Be careful," Merryn says. "It might be someone wanting to rob us."

Ding-dong. Ding-dong.

I switch on the light, open the door, and see a face I'd met just a few days before. It's our next-door neighbor, Amanda.

"I am *so* sorry to wake you at such an ungodly hour," she says as I usher her inside. "You remember me, from 294? Well, my husband, Ben, is away for work, and I've just come home from Manchester and spent the last forty minutes rummaging through my luggage trying to find my keys. Anyway, stupid me,

I've gone and lost them. My friend has a spare set but she's not answering her phone, and I've tried calling her so many times my battery is now flat. I'm cold, I'm tired, I'm hungry, but more importantly, I'm eight months pregnant and I desperately need to pee."

I have been reading a book on Englishness, and so far Amanda has broken all the rules. The English are aloof, the book says, but Amanda had greeted us cheerfully two days ago. The English won't tell you their names, according to the book, until they really know you—like, when you're about to marry their daughter—but Amanda had been quick to tell us hers. The English won't share much personal information with you, it says, but Amanda has just told me she needs to pee.

"Thank you, thank you, thank you," she says, holding her baby bump as she emerges from the bathroom, relieved. "I'll clean your clothes, I'll mop your floors—just tell me what I can do to repay you."

I assure Amanda there's no need for repayment, go and plug her phone in to charge, and get the spare bed ready should she need to stay. A few more phone calls and a taxi trip later, the spare keys are secured and we're laughing about it all the next day.

Merryn and I have lived in several homes and can't remember when meeting the neighbors had been so entertaining. And this unorthodox beginning starts something special between us. Amanda, Ben, Merryn, and I are soon sharing homemade pizzas on Friday nights, swapping keys, trading DVDs, and even safekeeping each other's valuables.

Merryn and I have found our first friends in Oxford.

For us, that is payment enough.

And all because Amanda lost her keys and needed to pee.

✳

Hi, Sheridan,

I'm so glad you and Merryn have made it to the UK, although I have to say that if your honeymoon feelings will be challenged by England's weather, they won't last long!

I have read your chapters and I love your writing. I particularly enjoyed your story about the lady on the bus who wanted to know if she was "all right." That is the periodically reignited scream of my heart and, I suspect, of many others. I would be more than happy to write an endorsement for your book, if you would like it. Any luck finding a publisher yet?

And when might you come and visit us? The pubs are waiting, and there is much metaphorical fat to be chewed.

I look forward to hearing from you. God bless.

Adrian Plass

✳

"So, what's your book about again?" she asks.

"It's called *More Than This*," I say, "and it's about God and the meaning of life."

"*Mmm*," she says, in a tone that sounds less than convinced.

I'm on the phone to the commissioning editor of one of the

UK's leading publishers. Having already turned me down via e-mail, the editor has granted me a phone call to try and persuade her about my book project.

"Adrian Plass has offered to endorse it," I say, bringing out my knock-down, fail-proof, let's-just-sign-the-contract-now piece of negotiating weaponry.

"That's good," she says, "but . . ."

I wait for a moment as the editor gathers her thoughts.

"Look," she says, "I know your books sold quite well in Australia; you obviously had a following there. You might have a good idea for this book, and well done for getting Adrian Plass's endorsement of it. But the fact is, you're unknown here in the UK, and us publishers . . ."

" . . . want authors with a profile," I say.

"It's the nature of the business, I'm afraid. Are you going to get into radio here? If so, why don't you come back to us when you're better known?"

✳

"So, tell me about your book idea," he says.

"It's called *More Than This*," I say. "It's about God and the meaning of life."

"*Mmm*," he says, tilting his head in a less-than-convinced fashion.

I'm out to lunch with another publisher—this one taking the time to drive out and see me. I've grown to like him quickly, and he's offered some valuable advice about the UK publishing industry. But as I tell him more about my book, I can see I'm making little headway.

"I've seen the books you released from your *Open House* show," he says. "I think something similar to those could be a better prospect. You are going to get back into radio, aren't you? You'll start a British version of *Open House* or something, right?"

*

"So, what kind of broadcasting are you passionate about?" he asks.

"I feel most alive when I'm talking about faith to a mainstream audience," I say. "Some of the most compelling radio I've done has been in conversation with atheists, New Agers, and other secular folks. That's what made the *Open House* concept work."

"*Mmm*," he says, in a noncommittal tone.

I'm in a meeting with executives from a Christian radio net-work. Their organization is doing some innovative things, but their style of broadcasting is very different to that pioneered in Australia, where the aim has been to reach both believing and unbelieving ears.

"We'd like to work with you," the general manager says, "but our mission is to super-serve our Christian audience rather than engage wider. That may take some adjustment for you."

"*Mmm*," I say, in a noncommittal tone.

*

"This job just keeps getting better," she says excitedly.

136

Merryn has returned from work with a smile on her face, bounding up our creaky stairs to find me in the study. She gives me a kiss, sits down on the spare bed, and faces me.

"I'm going to Australia," she says.

"Really? When?"

"In October, to collaborate on a medical trial with Adelaide University. I'll be able to take flights from there over to Sydney and up to Brisbane to see everybody. Cool, huh?"

"That's brilliant," I say, knowing a trip home so soon will delay Merryn's inevitable homesickness.

"And that's not all," she says. "I'm going to a conference next year."

"Great. Whereabouts?"

"In Norway."

"Of all places!"

"I think you'd better come with me, don't you?" she says playfully. "We could take a few days off and sail the fjords. Imagine the beauty you'll photograph there."

"This move is working out very well for you, isn't it, love?" I say.

"It really is," she says, her face a mixture of gratefulness and relief. "And how was your day?"

I glance at the ceiling, looking for the right words.

"Did you get much writing done?"

"Only one paragraph, actually. I had writer's block most of the day."

"You'll get there, love," she says.

"*Mmm,*" I say in a less-than-convinced tone.

———

*

Publishers want me on the radio so I can get "known," but once I'm back on air, I'll have little time to write. I'm working on a book I'm not sure anyone wants and being offered radio jobs that I won't like. The BBC hasn't returned my calls even though well connected people have recommended me. And for the first time in years, I don't know what I'm here to do—what dream I'm to pursue, what God has for me.

September 2011

"What an amazing day," I say.

"I feel so happy I could cry," Merryn says.

We sit in a dim sum restaurant in London's Soho—hardly the place to get misty-eyed. But the past twenty-four hours have felt like a divine gift—full of joy, grace, and surprise.

It had started last night when we'd taken our seats at the Queen's Theatre for a West End production of *Les Misérables*. The performance had been as brilliant as the story is moving: Valjean the criminal, who steals the Bishop's cutlery, but has his life redeemed when the Bishop conceals the robbery and offers him the candlesticks as well. We'd watched as this outcast became a man of mercy—protecting young Cosette and offering his nemesis, Javert, pity. It had been the right choice for our first West End show—a timeless story of a man touched by grace.

The British Museum was our focus today. Given its size, we

decided to start with the Egyptian galleries, then see the Rome and Greece rooms after that. We'd seen the famous Rosetta Stone that had broken the code of ancient hieroglyphics, and busts of Pharaohs dating to biblical times. An adjoining room led to the Assyrian gallery, and it was while wandering through there that our tour plans changed.

"This is the Black Obelisk," we heard an older man say, pointing to a statue while a small crowd looked on. "It records the triumphs of Shalmaneser III in the ninth-century BC. This ruler is mentioned in Second Kings 8, and if you look closely, just here, you'll see a carving of the Israelites paying him tribute."

The man explained the obelisk with such detail that, assuming he was a museum guide, we joined the group and followed him to the next exhibit.

"These panels decorated the walls of King Sennacherib's palace in Nineveh," he said, showing us a room of stone-carved battle scenes. "They depict his capture of Lachish in Judah in 701 BC, which is told in Second Kings, Second Chronicles, and Isaiah. These panels caused quite a stir when they were discovered in 1847, as they were the first archaeological confirmation of an event recorded in the Bible."

"And here is the Cylinder of Nabonidus," he said, taking us to another room where a small drum-like object etched with cuneiform script sat on a shelf. "Nabonidus was the father of King Belshazzar, who is mentioned in the book of Daniel. Secular scholars thought Belshazzar was a myth until this cylinder was discovered in southern Iraq in 1854. As these and other artifacts show, the Bible aligns with the records of history."

"Are you the couple Alan was expecting?" a friendly woman from the group soon asked me.

"Um, no," I said. "This is one of the museum's regular tours, right?"

"Oh no," she said. "This is a private tour. We're a church group."

I apologized profusely and said that we'd leave, but the woman insisted that we continue the tour and join them after lunch for a second one. And so this friendly group of Christians invited us into their day, showing us fascinating relics from the world of our faith, by a tour guide who turned out to be one of the world's most distinguished archaeologists. We couldn't have paid for a better experience.

"My feet are killing me now though," Merryn says as the dim sum waiter approaches.

"Here comes our dessert," I say. "After we eat, let's go back to the hotel for an early night. Who knows what's in store tomorrow."

The waiter sets down two mango puddings—our favorite dim sum dessert—and I notice that a couple at the next table are eyeing our dishes.

"Would you like to try it?" I say, handing my pudding over to them.

The woman initially declines, but after further encouragement picks up her spoon for a bite. And after flagging the waiter to bring a pudding for them, we all begin to chat.

"I'm Ali," the woman says a few minutes into the discussion. "I'm a psychotherapist."

"I'm Jeff," says the man. "I'm a professional nut job." We all laugh.

"With those occupations, you two must have some interesting conversations," I joke.

"Oh, we do," Ali says, laughing.

Jeff takes a roll of toilet paper from his backpack and tears off a long line of sheets to blow his flu-afflicted nose. "Well, we've all got stuff to deal with, haven't we?" he says.

"Yes, we do," Merryn says.

What ensues in the following moments again breaks all the rules of Englishness. The conversation between us grows surprisingly deep as Jeff and Ali start sharing their lives. They tell us about the books they've read and the self-improvement courses they've done in their search for growth and wholeness and the epiphanies they had on a recent retreat where they spent days on end in silence.

"What a fascinating journey you're on," I say later in the conversation. "I resonate with a lot of it as we're interested in spirituality too."

"Oh, what kind?" Ali says.

"Christian spirituality," I say, and Merryn and I share a little of how Jesus has changed our lives.

"It's so interesting you say that," Ali says, "because just this morning Jeff and I were discussing whether we should start thinking more about God."

"Really?" Merryn says.

"Yes, in fact, for the last couple of weeks I've been praying a prayer every morning. I don't even know where I got it from—perhaps it was from school. It goes something like this: 'Our Father who art in heaven, hallowed by your name . . .'"

"Your kingdom come, your will be done," I continue, "on earth as it is in heaven."

"You know it?" Ali says.

"It's a prayer Jesus taught his followers to pray. It's part of a famous talk he gave on a mountainside once to a crowd of people interested in spiritual living."

"Hey, do you two have anything planned this evening?" Jeff says as the waiter clears our empty dishes. "Maybe we could go for a drink and talk about God more."

And our feet suddenly don't feel so tired.

We walk a few streets to a Turkish tea house decked with draped walls, paisley cushions, candles on the tables, and the smell of incense. And as we sit on our cushions and sip green tea—and Jeff tends his flu with another toilet roll—Ali tells us things that she rarely tells others, Jeff shares the wounds he incurred as a child, and we talk about our wilderness experience and how we came to know Jesus and the difference he makes even if we don't always understand his ways.

"Isn't it amazing how we met tonight," Jeff says. "It's like it was all meant to be."

"I've got a feeling God arranged it," I say, and everyone agrees. "In fact, I think God arranged this because he wants you to know who he really is."

And we talk a little more about faith and belief—about Ali being a Jew and what her Jewishness means, and Jeff's aversion to church due to the hypocrisy he's seen. And it starts to get late, so we all swap numbers and talk about planning to meet again soon. And before we leave I suggest that we pray, and there in the tea house, with the cushions and incense, we all bow our heads without a care of who sees, and I thank God for orchestrating our serendipitous meeting, and for Jeff and for Ali, these new friends we've made. And I thank God that he loves them and wants them to know him, and I ask God to heal them and guide them and bless them. And Ali says "wow" and Jeff starts to cry, and we all know that God has been with us in the tea house tonight.

And as our bus pulls back into Oxford the next day, Merryn and I come home feeling touched by grace—by a God who prompts strangers in museums to include us, and who links us with new friends in Soho restaurants.

And we start the new week feeling a bit more resurrected.

*

"What's your background again?" he says.

I tell the well-spoken man on the phone about my broadcast career, my previous books, and some other accomplishments in Australia.

"Mmm," he says, in a tone that's difficult to read.

Thanks to yet another recommendation from a well-connected friend, I'm finally talking to a producer at the BBC about contributing to their national programs.

"I'm afraid," the producer says, cutting to the chase, "there's little chance of us using you on Radio 4, as only highly-known faith leaders or journalists present those segments. And there's only a slim possibility we'd use you on Radio 2, as why would we choose someone new to the country over a presenter who's been here for years?"

If I was in your place, I think to myself, *I'd probably say the same thing.*

∗

"And what are your qualifications for writing a book like that?" he asks. "I take it you have formal training in theology or philosophy?"

I'm on the second floor of Blackwell's bookshop, having coffee with an Oxford theologian. My two small degrees pale before his numerous PhDs, and even the significant research I mention doesn't seem to convince him of my worthiness to write my book. Or at least that's how this under-confident soul interprets his response.

Maybe he's right? I wonder, as I ride home later.

In a university town like Oxford, where it can feel like even the garbage collectors all have PhDs, you soon become aware of your credentials.

And maybe you just don't have the credentials, Sheridan, in this city of experts.

∗

"Excuse me," I say to a couple walking toward us. "What is that you've just seen?"

"It's an old nunnery," the girl says, glancing back at the crumbling walls. "It's worth a look while there's still light, if you can."

Merryn and I have had dinner at the Trout Inn, a seventeenth-century ivy-covered pub on the River Thames just north of the city, made famous by Colin Dexter's *Inspector Morse* novels. Crossing the Godstow Bridge for a post-dinner walk, we'd seen the remains of what is the old Abbey, though hadn't yet seen the sign.

"Are you Australian?" I ask, noting the girl's accent.

"We are," she says. "We're on holidays from Sydney."

With a city in common we start talking suburbs and find we haven't lived far apart. And the couple, it so happens, works for a Christian organization, and we discover we have mutual friends.

"You know," the girl says, "I recognize your voice."

"Well, I used to host this radio show called . . ."

"You're Sheridan Voysey," she says. "I knew it. I used to listen to you all the time."

The girl and her husband then recount some of their favorite shows before saying how great Leigh is doing as the new *Open House* host. And when we say good-bye and Merryn and I walk toward the old nunnery, I reflect on the irony of meeting a listener so far from home.

Chance encounters with listeners like this used to make me happy, like the time we randomly called a tour group in Turkey and put a girl to air who just happened to be a fan of the show. But as we walk along the walls of Godstow Abbey, I feel a wave of sadness now. Conversations like this, even though encouraging, are reminders of what I've left behind.

I wake up some mornings . . .

I later write in my journal,

and the world seems full of possibilities. But on other days it feels like my life is over. Like I no longer matter. Like what is lost is gone forever.

The feelings of insignificance have been the most crushing, picking away at my soul as if to reduce me to ash. "You had an audience of thousands," a little voice says, "but now no one cares what you say. Once applauded, you're now forgettable; spiritually impotent, professionally irrelevant. You used to make a difference, but now you lack influence."

Ah, influence, maybe you became an idol—judging by my response since you've left. While I had you I felt valuable, important, or at the very least, helpful. I'm disappointed how much I miss you when Jesus cared little for you.

And these feelings of jealousy that now rear their head—for the authors and speakers who succeed while I don't. Ugly, this is. Just ugly. I despise my ugly envy.

Masculinity—now that's taken a hit, as Merryn earns the money while I put in a load of washing. I feel it most acutely when people ask why we're here. "For your work?" they say, looking at me. "For hers," I reply, pointing to Merryn. And when they ask what I'm doing and I say, "Writing a book," you can tell some are thinking, *Another wannabe author.* And part of me wants to tell them, "I was important once, you know," and "I've written books and had my own radio show." And then I feel pathetic for such self-consciousness.

The exhaustion is the interesting one—how fatigued I feel. It took years to build what I had—the credibility, the contacts, the "influence," the "profile"—and I feel weary at having to build it again. But do I really have to? Need to? That's the thing—I don't know.

I don't know who I am anymore.

"Am I a broadcaster who writes, or a writer who also speaks? Am I a journalist, an apologist, or a pastor? I've been a bit of each. But who am I now? Who am I to become?

Lord?

Lord!

Please answer.

October 2011

Hundreds fill the church auditorium. The music is loud and vibrant. Projectors display lyrics onto the walls and the singing is exuberant. Some close their eyes, some shout their praise, some dance in the aisles, some embrace and pray. Children near the stage wave colorful flags while their parents raise their hands to heaven.

After an hour of singing, the praise band take their seats, and the pastor gets ready to preach his sermon. But before he does, a man with blond-grey hair steps onto the stage to speak.

"I met someone before the service started," he says, looking over the congregation. "I think your name was Sheridan. I feel the Lord wants to say something to you today."

We have been on a mission to find a new church and have visited a number so far. We've sat in the stalls of Christ Church Cathedral for a traditional service with hymns and choir, visited the evangelical St. Ebbe's Anglican for a dose of scholarly biblical teaching, spent a few Sundays at the dynamic St. Aldate's, where each service is full to overflowing, and enjoyed the hospitality at little Magdalen Road Church, where we were invited for lunch the moment we walked in. And today we're paying a visit to Oxford Community Church—a lively crowd who seek God with a passion.

"The Lord wants to say this to you . . ."

We'd spoken to Simon, the man on the stage, just briefly on arrival this morning. Now he has our attention, though we're not without caution, as we've had "prophecies" given to us before. During IVF, a well-meaning friend told us she'd had a vision of us having a baby boy. During our adoption phase, another friend had shared her vision of a jigsaw puzzle coming together—God fitting us with an adoptive child in due time. Then there was John's urgent prayer for me at the radio station that day, and the image of a womb given to those at the prayer meeting last year. All of these experiences came wrapped in love, but the prophesied baby never came.

Still, didn't Saint Paul say not to treat prophecies with contempt? Didn't he say to test them and hold to those that were true?

"You haven't seen everything the Lord has planned for you," Simon says from the stage. "God has something in store; you just haven't seen it yet. So persevere. He's brought you here for a reason."

*

"How's the book coming along?" he asks as I return from the bar with our drinks.

"Oh, it ticks along," I say, pushing his beer across the table.

"Cheers," he says.

"Cheers."

My friend Darren is in Oxford for a few weeks, working on his PhD. We first met years ago when we collaborated on a radio project tackling child poverty and became good friends during our trips to the developing world. Darren was one of the first people I'd opened up to after the horrors of last December. As I slide onto the red chesterfield bench behind our table at The Grapes pub, I'm thankful he's here.

"Actually," I say, "I've been reading through my old journals today."

"Looking for material?" he says.

"Yeah. Most of what I write is first scribbled in those notebooks. It's the stuff you find in between those notes, though, that is the most telling."

"What did you find?"

"It can be encouraging," I say, "to find a prayer written in one journal answered in another. Today, for instance, I found a prayer I wrote years ago asking God to make me a writer."

"Wow," Darren says, "there's a prayer that was answered."

"And over time you see certain themes develop in your life. The ideas that have dominated my writing and speaking in recent years I find first mentioned in my journals over a decade ago. I sometimes wonder if each of us has just a few key themes in our lives that we spiral back to."

"What would they be for you?"

"On the personal front," I say, "it's intriguing to see how much responsibility recurs in the early journals. And love. I would take on too much responsibility, thinking I was being 'loving' when I was really just being a rescuer. Thankfully that theme falls quiet in later journals once I addressed the problem, but it still pops up from time to time."

"And anything else?"

"Well, yes," I say. "The theme of identity. It's there in the early journals, partly because I was writing about it then, but also because I've often wrestled with it—knowing who I am. It's a theme that's returned recently, to be honest. This move has triggered the old questions in a new way."

"As a result of leaving *Open House*?"

"And the other public roles," I say. "I don't like to think it's true, but I wonder now how much my self-worth has been based on being 'popular' and 'influential'—even though I really wasn't much of either. There are far more influential people out there than me."

"Still, a lot of people listened to you," Darren says, "and were blessed by your work."

"It's nice when God uses you to help people," I say. "I did get some lovely e-mails."

A few moments pass as we sip our drinks, then Darren says, "I went through something similar when I left the band."

Darren had once been the lead singer of a full-time Christian band. For seven years they toured Australia, living by faith, visiting hundreds of towns, and performing at churches, schools, and anywhere else that would have them. It was a grueling few years of long drives and late nights.

"And that schedule finally caught up with me," he says. "I had a burnout of sorts and had to leave the band just as we were finalizing our next album. After the hours I'd invested in that record—all the writing, arranging, and recording—I was devastated.

"Anyway, they finished the album without me, and one day I got a copy in the mail. I put the CD in my player and started to listen. It had turned out pretty well. Then I started reading the album's liner notes."

"And?"

"I wasn't there," he says. "Page after page I read, and I wasn't even mentioned."

I shake my head in disbelief.

"Finally I came to a paragraph on the last page where a raft of people was thanked. And there, right at the end, was my name. I'd made it just before the band's appreciation for Daihatsu trucks and Chupa Chups."

We laugh in a way you can only do when the sting of injury has passed.

"After all those years pouring my life into the band, I had been reduced to nothing. I think it was then that I learned something profound."

I lean in to hear.

"I was bedridden, exhausted, and had nothing left to offer the world. I could accomplish nothing to make God love me or feel proud of me. All I had left, in fact, was God's grace—which is all I'd ever had in the first place."

*

"How great is the love the Father has lavished on us, that we should be called children of God," says Saint John. "And that is what we are." My role, position, or status may change, but this identity will remain—I am child of God. I am child of God whether I succeed or fail. I am a child of God whether applauded or forgotten.

Some lessons, Lord, need to be relearned. I'm significant to you, and that will never change.

*

It's dark now, and the colorful flowerpots along Broad Street bathe in the soft light of its old streetlamps. I unlock my bike from the racks near Blackwell's bookshop and walk it slowly up the street—past students, tourists, and ivy-covered buildings, past the medieval walls of Balliol College, turning left at Debenham's into Cornmarket mall, where Shakespeare used to lodge at the Crown Tavern. The shops and stores are more familiar to me now, as is the little intersection of paths where I now pause.

The day had begun with loud songs and raised hands—another service spent with my charismatic friends. The sermon this morning had been about Peter walking on water and how Jesus calls us all to step out of the familiar and into his miraculous care. I had then visited the Sheldonian Theatre with a friend to hear two eminent philosophers debate the existence of God. The afternoon had been spent in a cafe talking theology with strangers, then at the Eagle and Child pub, Lewis and Tolkien's old haunt.

A well-known musician had been performing at the Cathedral tonight, so we'd dropped in there after dinner. And as we'd stepped outside into the giant quadrangle, a brilliant white moon shone in the steel blue sky and the bell tower's reflection had rippled in the pond and the stars had twinkled—making the whole night magical.

And now I pause in Cornmarket mall, standing at the crossroads, looking. Down the path to my right stands Wesley Memorial Church—its gothic tower shining, its spire piercing the sky. And down the path on my left is Exeter College—its own steeple glowing resplendent tonight.

And it strikes me that I've seen the best of Oxford today—its splendor, majesty, and soul. This is a city of both old and new churches, of musical performances and debates in theatres, where deep conversations start between strangers, of sparkling stars and luminous spires.

And though sometimes it feels like a wilderness to me—a place of questions, confusion, and uncertainty—today I glimpse something different in Oxford. For Merryn it has become a promised land. Perhaps it could become that for me.

Because there's a story on each corner of Oxford's main streets. Every sandstone brick of its walls is soaked with the conversations of the greats.

I get on my bicycle and pass by Christ Church meadow.

Riding in our city—our home among the spires.

———

7

Making Love in Paris

December 2011

Padlocks. Hundreds of them. Perhaps even thousands. They are clasped to the rails of the Pont des Arts Bridge. Each bronze lock is inscribed with two names. And upon each little lock a wish has been placed. They hang along the walkway like the yellow leaves of autumn—like a wall of autumn leaves one hopes will never fall.

There is a romantic quality to Paris's Pont des Arts Bridge. On a clear day painters and artists set up their easels and sketchpads to capture its views of the city and the River Seine. In summer, picnic rugs are spread on its planks, and groups of friends sit down to share wine and laughter. At night the Pont des Arts becomes magical as floodlights illuminate the domed French Academy at one end and the Louvre Museum at the other.

But it is for these padlocks that the bridge has become best known of late. No one quite knows where the idea came from. Some trace it to a recent novel by Italian writer Federico Moccia, although the locks appeared elsewhere in Europe some years before. Whatever its origin, the ritual is quaint. Two sweethearts meet at the Pont des Arts. They take a padlock on which they've written or engraved their names, weave its hook through the wire mesh of the bridge's fence, and lock it tight. And then, as the sun sets over Paris, the couple take the padlock's key and throw it into the Seine as a symbolic gesture of their eternal love.

I wonder as I ponder these thousands of locks what really is being thrown to the waters. Surely it is loneliness and insecurity (including the loneliness of promiscuity) and the anxiety of romantic ambiguity and impermanence. Deep down all of us want someone with whom we're locked, clasped, and bonded. Deep down we all need exclusivity—a lover who has bound themselves to us and thrown away the key.

But then I wonder how many locks clicked with not just a wish but a promise. Not just a hope but a pledge. Not just a dream but a vow.

For eternal love is nothing if not committed.

*

A bus to London, then a train to Paris—it took only a few hours to reach the city of love. This new proximity is exciting for us

Australians, as France has always been on the "other side" of the world. From Gare du Nord station we'd found our accommodation on Rue Rodier and climbed the tiny spiral stairs to our fourth-floor apartment. And after a walk around the streets eyeing the boulangeries and patisseries and the ladies in fur coats carrying poodles in their handbags, we have dressed up to celebrate at a small nearby restaurant.

"Happy anniversary," I say, raising my champagne flute.

"Fifteen years," she says, clinking my glass, "and never a cross word."

Merryn's grandfather had said that phrase on his sixtieth anniversary, bringing howls of laughter from those who knew better—the bickering between him and Merryn's grandma renowned. Since then it had become one of those shorthand phrases a couple has that needs no explanation.

"Wasn't our honeymoon the best?" Merryn says wistfully.

"In that '74 Corona and that two-man tent," I say.

"Remember me emptying all that pepper into our dinner and you trying so hard to eat it?"

"Remember the night we got mauled by mosquitoes, and I sprayed your backside with repellent so you wouldn't get bitten going to the toilet?"

"Remember that old camera I had with a matchstick for a shutter button?

"Remember getting frustrated with me flicking between radio stations?"

"Remember the car windshield getting smashed by that rock?"

"Remember the daily chocolate Paddle Pops?"

———

"Good memories," she says, smiling.

Our entree of escargot arrives. We hold each shell with the special tongs and extract each snail with a liberal coating of garlic butter.

"Remember our first flat, on Cavendish Road," I say, "with our second-hand couches and our borrowed TV?"

"We felt so grown up and free," she says.

"And then buying that place on Maryborough Terrace, with the 50s-style kitchen and the worn-out carpet? And painting and renovating and making it our own."

"I designed the kitchen and you painted the walls."

"We didn't know we could do it until we tried."

We eat the escargot quietly in recollection, then Merryn says, "I didn't know who I wanted to be back then, but I knew I wanted to be with you. I always knew our life would be an adventure together."

Some risks had been taken on the largely illegible French menu, so we're glad when our mains arrive looking good—chicken medallions for Merryn in a creamy sauce; the lamb for me in some exotic jus.

"I think I was most proud of us when we moved to Perth," Merryn says. "We moved so far away from home and proved we could make it on our own."

"Perhaps that's when we really became a *couple*," I say.

"That's where we started facing some crises together."

"That's where we learned to handle our disputes—staying seated on that couch and talking things through when all we wanted to do was leave the room."

"That's where you barred me from talking to car salesmen," she says, smiling.

"Your declaration of love for that red Mazda killed all negotiation on its price."

"But you can thank me for getting published."

"I wouldn't have pitched that first magazine article without you," I say. "I didn't have the confidence."

"See?" she says. "I had other endearing qualities."

"You did," I say as we laugh. "And you still do." Merryn's black blouse augments her dark brown hair beautifully tonight. Her smile still lights up the room.

I top up our glasses and we hold hands across the table, breaking only when our waitress arrives with dessert. To me it's unthinkable to visit Paris without ordering crème brûlée. The caramelized top of this one is perfect, its vanilla filling silky smooth.

"Thanks for going to Sydney," I say, "when part of you wanted to return to Brisbane."

"Thanks for coming to England," she says, "when you wanted to stay in Australia."

"We've had some good times already, haven't we?"

"Remember driving to Uluru?"

"Remember climbing Machu Picchu?"

"Remember that time at Lord Howe Island when we . . ."

"Shh!" she tells me. "Someone might overhear you." And we giggle.

"I love you, you know."

"I love you too."

———

"64."

"64."

Shared memories, stories, houses, bodies, shared hopes, dreams, and crises. Shared words, phrases, codes, and jokes. Shared secrets no one else can know. The wonder of marriage is that two lives combine, like a thread linking different colored fabrics. Fifteen years ago Merryn and I opened our arms wide and granted each other access, and as a result we've become intertwined—through our playing, praying, sleeping, and weeping, through silly songs in the morning and silly dances in the evening; through bearing each other's burdens, supporting each other's ventures, and laughing so hard together we've doubled over in stitches. We've entrusted each other with our most vulnerable selves—our sins, our fears, our regrets. We've entrusted each other with our loftiest dreams—aspirations others would probably laugh at. And we've entrusted each other with that ultimate vulnerability—the unguarded state of nakedness. For fifteen years we have woven those threads and created something sacred.

A memory floats to mind as we finish the champagne, say "au revoir" to the waitress, and leave the restaurant for the bustling street. It's from a while back, perhaps 2003, when we'd started wondering if IVF was worth a try.

"In-vitro fertilization can strain a relationship," the counselor had said as we sat in the beige discussion room of the hospital.

"We've heard the drugs can cause emotional upsets for the woman," I'd said. "Is that the stress you mean?"

"Yes," she'd replied, "but not just that. You'll have many decisions to make if you go ahead, like how many rounds of IVF you'll attempt and what you'll do if you don't succeed. Some couples find this the most difficult part. It can lead to many disagreements."

"We've talked about that," Merryn had said, "and have decided we won't let IVF come between us. Our marriage is more important than having a child."

With that, the counselor had slumped with relief and dropped her "objective" social worker stance. "I'm so glad you just said that," she'd said, exhaling. "Only last week a woman told me in front of her husband that if she didn't have a baby their marriage was through."

While cooing couples glow as they throw their keys to the Seine, not every rendezvous on the Pont des Arts Bridge goes to plan. Some uncoordinated couples misjudge the throw, their key landing on the path running along the river beneath them. And Parisian authorities, like those in other affected cities, have wondered what to do with this metallic graffiti. In many cases the answer is a pair of bolt cutters, a tradesman prizing off all but the oldest and most notable locks.

And so, sadly, some of the autumn leaves on the Pont des Arts Bridge will fall. For some the romance will end when an uninterested partner scuttles under the bridge, retrieves the key, and sets themselves free from their "everlasting" bond. Other couples will be prized apart by an outside force—a lover, a career, the pursuit of a child at any cost. What God locks together let no man or woman separate. The result is only ever heartbreak.

———

But thank God some padlocks go unbroken—the key long forgotten, competing forces withstood. A little weathered from the storms and tarnished in places, they remain locked, clasped, bonded, wedded—life's trials faced together, their eternal love committed.

Two sweethearts stroll home to their fourth-floor apartment. Lock the door and celebrate their bond.

January 2007

"When will you go back to Australia, Daddy?" she asks me.

"Tomorrow we fly to Indonesia," I say somberly, "then we go home a few days later."

"Maybe we'll see each other again one day," she says, tears welling in her eyes.

And I want to shout, "Yes, Riza, we will—we *will* see each other again." But the words don't come out of my mouth.

The day has felt like a dream—wistful, floaty, otherworldly. This is due partly to us being in the Philippines, in Bacolod City on the island of Negros, though there are other reasons for the feelings. Today we've met Riza, our sponsor child, in person. In just a few short hours I've fallen in love. In one more hour I'll be heartbroken.

Merryn and I had taken our seats in the little restaurant at lunchtime. A few minutes later, workers from the sponsorship agency had walked in, accompanied by fifteen-year-old Riza. She wore a pair of blue jeans, a pink belt, an apricot T-shirt, and her long brown hair in a ponytail. In her hand was a plastic bag containing every letter we'd written to her over the last eight years of sponsoring her education. The moment we saw her our hearts melted. The moment she saw us she burst into tears.

"I have prayed to God to be able to meet you," she'd said. "Today God has answered my prayers."

Riza's father is a welder, her mother a homemaker, and they live in a one-room shack shared with two dogs and two cats. At night Riza sleeps on the bed with her mother while her father sleeps on the sofa. The electricity in her home powers a light bulb and a radio, and her wardrobe consists of a cardboard box holding a white dress and her school uniform—her only other clothes.

"We've brought you some presents," we'd said to Riza.

"I've brought you one too," she'd said to us.

Her present had been a handmade folder full of pictures of her, her family, and her friends, decorated with stickers, drawings, and glitter. We'd brought a book about Australian animals and a small girl's watch in her favorite color, blue. She'd quickly strapped it on.

"Did you bring me a copy of your book, Daddy?" she'd said excitedly.

Daddy. Mommy. Riza's titles for us are touching. She has her own fine family but considers us her sponsor parents.

"How do you know about my book?" I'd said, taken by surprise.

"You told me about it, here," she'd said, pulling out the appropriate letter. It was as if she'd memorized every one of our words.

I'd apologized and said that I'd get a book sent, and she'd said she'd like that because she was proud I wrote books. And we'd told her about Australia, and she'd taught us some Filipino words, and then we'd all taken a drive to a local resort. And there we'd wandered around the gardens, hot springs, and pools. She'd pointed out the flowers and how pretty they looked. And I'd wondered how many Australian teenagers cared about flowers. Or scenery. Or butterflies. Or the other natural wonders that caught Riza's eye.

And I'd wondered about these feelings that were now swarming in my soul. Feelings I'd never felt before. Feelings for this sweet girl.

I had met nice kids, cute kids, polite teenagers before. I had already met children in poverty, and in the coming years I would meet many more. I'd even met other children we sponsored—that had been fun but nothing like this. These weren't romantic notions of cuteness, rescue, or being appreciated, I don't think. These feelings were unique.

Because suddenly I wanted to protect Riza with all the strength I had. I wanted to vet all future boyfriends and help her choose the best. I wanted to put her through college and see her graduate. I wanted to watch her get her first job. I wanted to be there on her wedding day.

Suddenly I wanted to adopt Riza and whisk her far away. Take her home. Claim her as my own.

Get a grip, Sheridan. She's not yours, you know.

But for some mysterious reason, I wished she was.

And now we sit in the back of a minivan taking the bumpy road back to Bacolod City. Tomorrow Merryn and I fly out to Manila, then on to Indonesia, and after a few days work, make the four-thousand-mile journey home. There is so much distance between us and Riza. The plane flights alone cost thousands of dollars—impossible for her to afford and prohibitive for us to consider often. She has no phone, so we can't call her. But after today letters will never be enough. I feel like I'm about to lose her.

"I really like my watch, Daddy," she says, looking at it under the rushing street lights.

"I love it because it came from the two of you."

"This has been one of the best days of my life," I say.

"Me too," she says.

We pull in to the parking lot of the Bacolod Hotel and climb out of the van with our bags. A rickshaw driver is waiting to take Riza home. We shake hands with the agency workers, thankful for their part in our special day, and then we take Riza in our arms and hug her tight. Then we hug her again. Then we say good-bye, her glittery folder safe in my hands.

Riza walks to the rickshaw. We wave and turn away. Then we both burst into tears.

And then Riza runs over and hugs us once more.

We hide our red eyes from the hotel staff, dash through the foyer to the vacant lift, then rush through the hallway to our room. I collapse on the bed and weep for an hour, then for a second hour. And again the next day. Merryn has never seen me like this.

I don't understand it.

I write in my journal.

———

I have nothing to compare these feelings to. Is this what it's like to lose someone close? The grief is so deep—I hate it; it hurts. But is it somehow good? Merryn has always been the one with parental desires. I was the partner less affected. But then I meet Riza and . . . She's someone else's daughter, not mine—get that clear. But I don't know any other way to describe what I'm feeling than to say it feels like I'm leaving someone precious behind.

Riza feels like the daughter I'll never have.

December 2011

A few minutes' walk from our apartment on Rue Rodier is the colorful district of Montmartre. With our dark jackets and new scarves, we look like true Europeans, walking the cobblestone streets past its old boutique-style shops. Think *Amélie* or *Moulin Rouge*—both movies were filmed here. With a touch of mist we could be characters in one of Henri Cartier-Bresson's classic black-and-white photographs.

A mix of nationalities crowd the sidewalks. There's graffiti on the walls and small groups gather round upturned cardboard boxes to lose their money to wily street gamblers. Cancan dancers still perform at the Elysee Montmartre Theatre, Paris's red light district is just down the road, and music stores and nightclubs reflect the region's bohemian roots. Originally a working class village offering cheap wine and rent, Montmartre was once the haunt of the world's greatest artists. Picasso, Monet, and Matisse lived and painted here, as did Renoir, Dali, Mondrian, and Van Gogh.

But while Montmartre's heritage includes the artistic and the decadent, it also includes the saintly and the devout. It is a little mountain with a rich religious history.

Originally a site of worship to Mars and Mercury, for hundreds of years since it has been a place of Christian significance—a high and holy mountain devoted to Jesus. The name Montmartre—"the mountain of the martyr"—is in honor of Saint Denis, the first Bishop of Paris, who was likely decapitated here in AD 250, and over the centuries many notable names have trekked up these slopes to pray. Saints Germain, Bernard, and Vincent de Paul worshipped on this mountain, as well as Joan of Arc, Dante Alighieri, Thomas Aquinas, and Francis de Sales.

One historic Montmartre event captures my imagination. In 1534 the famed saint Ignatius of Loyola climbed this hill with six of his friends. Here they dedicated themselves to God and each other and founded a movement of considerable influence—the Society of Jesus, better known as the Jesuits. Their vision was simple: small communities of Christians living together and serving others for the glory of God. Ignatius and his friends started schools, helped the poor, and invented the guided retreat for spiritual renewal. They sought the salvation of the world through the transformation of the heart. Jesuit communities were soon started around the world.

How many lives have been changed through the vows made by Ignatius and his friends on this mountain? And how many more by other saints like them? For God has always dispensed his love through committed individuals. It is his grace we receive as they lay their hands on our lives.

———

And I think of all the saints who blessed Merryn and me during those hard years in the wilderness—the holy friends with consecrated hands who bestowed God's blessings upon our heads.

Like Darren, my singer friend, who drove for hours to see me when I needed to talk. Like Peter and Jason, my old mates from Brisbane, with whom I spent some important weekends walking in the woods. Like the small inner circle who prayed and pleaded to God as we entered the final stages of our journey. Like the little band of friends we met with every Friday night who became our spiritual family.

That little Friday night group . . . how precious it was.

We called ourselves the Croydon Centre for Spiritual Enlightenment in jest. There was no centre, just a lounge room. No enlightened gurus, just us. We did meet in Croydon, though, and this little gathering did change us spiritually. Our weekly routine was simple: we ate together, shared our weeks, read the Bible, and prayed. Plenty of church fellowship groups do the same four things, but this one . . . this one had something special. Its atmosphere was accepting. Its warmth was tangible.

We were all so different. There was Ben the lawyer, Heidi the writer, Ali the marketer, and Mel the missionary from China. There was Ella the physiotherapist, Adam the banker, Sam the musician, Merryn the statistician, and Natalie the legal editor and activist. We all had different personalities, callings, and political leanings, but we liked, loved, and listened to each other, seeking Jesus together through life's joys and trials.

Some Fridays we celebrated—like the time Ben started his own law firm and Heidi got her book deal and Ali got the all clear after her battle with cancer. Every Friday we laughed—like the time we nearly wet ourselves looking at those funny photos on the computer. And some Fridays were somber as we bore each other's sadness—like when Mel's singleness got her down or our infertility became too much to bear. There were times when Merryn and I could no longer pray, and these Friday night friends filled the gap. Like the four men in the Gospel story who lowered their paralytic friend through the roof to Jesus, this little group brought us to God when all we could do was lie motionless.

Like chronic illness, unwanted singleness, and other life statuses that deviate from the "norm," childlessness can bring isolation. Your friends start experiencing things you cannot share; their interests shift, your conversations change, and you begin to lose things in common. Some people are tactless, gushing for hours about their babies; for a time you must avoid them to cope with the pain. Merryn stopped attending baby showers and still skips church on Mother's Day. Infertility can remove you from community.

Ironically, people's concern can result in isolation too. We heard of one family who chose not to invite us for dinner, thinking their having children would make us sad. On more than one occasion, close friends concealed their pregnancies from us, wanting to protect us, but we just felt distanced. Others have felt selfish around us for wanting a second child when we can't even have one. Compassion can be a complex business.

The faith element can add another layer of difficulty. How do you tell the well-meaning lady who wants to pray for your fertility (because the doctors told *her* she'd never conceive and God gave her a *miracle* baby) that, no, you'd rather she didn't pray? Your reluctance can be interpreted as a lack of faith (when it's actually protection from more raised-and-dashed hopes). And the story's too exhausting to go into again, so you can't vindicate your spirituality.

The fact is, however, that few will be able to get it right. Because you feel sad when a friend tells you they're pregnant and sad when they keep it from you; you want to share your friend's joy but avoid the pain it will recall; you want people to pray—but only certain prayers at certain times; you need a community to be part of, but you also need your space.

And this awkward state will be your life for a while—these emotional complexities are your lot. And while the pain will ease as the balm of time works, you may always feel a little misfitted to the world.

And that's why I'm thankful for holy friends with consecrated hands who mediate God's blessings through their steadfast presence—who come to your side when you need to talk, who pray and plead in your moment of need, who dig through roofs to get you to Jesus, who share their lives with you and invite you to share yours, and give you space when you need it.

Even when things get a little awkward.

God has always dispensed his love through committed friendship.

Courses of stairs line Montmartre hill like streams trickling down from its peak. We take a steep set on the right-hand side, hedged by wrought-iron lamps, shrubs, and trees, then make our ascent up the steps. Reaching the crest, we walk to a platform and feast on views of Paris that stretch for miles. This skyline, however, is not our main interest. Montmartre's real glory stands behind us.

Even on this overcast day, the Sacré-Coeur Basilica gleams. It rests atop Montmartre like an ornate crown, its ivory-white domes bejeweled with sculptures and crosses. We climb the polished steps and enter through a creaky door into its large, hushed sanctuary. And within seconds ours eyes, like everyone else's, are transfixed by the image on the ceiling.

"Wow," I say.

"Wow," Merryn says.

"Wow," says a girl walking in behind us.

The figure towers above the altar in a rich mosaic of blue and gold. Glowing robe. Golden heart. Piercing eyes. Outstretched arms.

"Look at Jesus," the girl says in wonder.

We can hardly see anything else.

Merryn and I take a seat in one of the wooden pews to contemplate the picture. As if peeling back the veil to an unseen realm, it evokes wonder, awe, reverence.

Jesus stands in the centre of the piece. Rays of gold emanate from his body, commanding the gaze of all others. Mary is on the left, beside and below him, her adoring face fixed on her son. Beside Mary is a tiny Pope Leo XIII offering Jesus a globe of the world. Behind Pope Leo are representatives of every culture, and behind them are other popes and cardinals.

To the right of Jesus stands the archangel Michael and Joan of Arc with her arms stretched wide. Nestled between them is "France incarnate"—a white-gowned woman offering Jesus her crown—with French royalty, government, and church leaders behind her.

In the heavens on our left the apostles Peter, Paul, and John are joined by a host of saints, including Augustine, Gertrude, Francis of Assisi, and Ignatius of Loyola. In the heavens on our right the saints of France look on, including Denis, Genevieve, Margaret-Mary, and Vincent de Paul. And if you look a little longer you'll notice a red-and-gold line connecting Jesus with a dove and a mysterious crowned figure. Here is the One God—Father, Son, and Holy Spirit—being worshipped by France, heaven, and all of creation.

A procession of people circuit Sacré-Coeur's outer rim, viewing its chapels and works of art. We leave our seats and join them for a while, and as we walk slowly around I'm struck by something: people in this church are actually worshipping.

I've always thought it a tragedy that one can visit the great cathedrals of the world and not be moved to worship. We visit these places on the tourist trail, marvel at the architecture, admire the stained-glass windows, and enjoy the pretty flickering candles before taking a photo for posterity and exiting via the gift shop. But how often do such "holy" places arrest us with a desire to worship the Holy One? I wasn't so moved visiting Notre Dame Cathedral yesterday, nor at John Calvin's old church, Saint Pierre's, while in Geneva. Even my response at Saint Peter's was more aesthetic in nature. But something is different here at Montmartre. People kneel in the aisles. Some recite prayers. Others read their Bibles. All gaze at Jesus.

As we complete our circuit of Sacré-Coeur, I tell Merryn I need to stay a little longer. I stroll over to the central section roped off for worshippers, pass the usher, and walk down the aisle to the mosaic above the altar.

And sit at the feet of Jesus.

Gentle murmurs echo in the basilica like soft angelic voices. And there in my pew I join the angels, the saints, the cardinals, and the apostles to contemplate the One in the glowing robe with the piercing eyes.

Here is the Sacré-Coeur—the "sacred heart"—the heart that is both human and divine. Here is One who healed sickness with a touch, expelled demons with a word, fed a multitude with scraps of bread, and settled storms by command—yet sweated and thirsted and got dirt in his sandals and wept and got tired like you and I do.

Here is One who entered the wilderness and faced its temptations—to turn stones into bread, seeking his own fulfillment; to leap from the temple, seeking fame and applause; to bow to the devil, seeking power and control—emerging unsullied but able to sympathize with our weakness.

Here is One who has felt our isolation—the loneliness and loss, the alienation. Rejected by priests and hunted by politicians, his neighbors even drove him out of town. Judas betrayed him. Peter denied him. His family once told him he was mad. In his hour of need all his friends fled. Crowds that once praised him later called for his death.

And was it the silence of God he experienced in Gethsemane—when he pleaded for his life to be spared? He prayed three times with such anguish he sweated blood; even an angel couldn't console his distress.[1] Yet there was no voice from heaven like there was at his baptism, no thundery words as there were at his transfiguration. Only silence.

"Yet I want your will to be done, not mine."[2]

What dreams did you relinquish to submit to that will, Jesus? What hopes were deferred for you? You stayed single in a culture that raised eyebrows at that status. To die without children was considered a tragedy. Did that human side of you wish for things to be different? Deep down did you long for a family?

"Who are my mother and my brothers?" he says.[3]

That's right—you widened the boundaries of what we call a family.

"Whoever does God's will is my brother and sister and mother."

Whoever does God's will—a family not of bloodline but of faith. Including, for us, those Friday night friends and sweet Filipino girls with ponytails?

"Yet when his life is made an offering for sin, he will have many descendants."[4]

No biological children for you, but many spiritual "descendants." Perhaps we can be spiritual fathers and mothers in the faith too.

Here is One who came and rubbed shoulders with us, experiencing the cruelty of our unjust world. A world where unwanted babies are found on rubbish dumps while childless couples wait. A world where a sinless man can be condemned to death by those he came to save.

He was taken and tried in an unjust court, on trumped-up charges with put-up witnesses. He was put in a fancy-dress gown with a crown of thorns, then was beaten, spat on, and ridiculed. He was taken to the town square and publicly whipped. He was taken to a hill and stripped bare. And there he was nailed to two bits of wood, like a butterfly pinned to a board.

What were you feeling, Lord? What agony was in your mind and heart?

"My God, my God," he cries, "why have you abandoned me?"[5]

You felt the absence of God too. And like us, you questioned why.

"Why are you so far away when I groan for help? Every day I call to you, my God, but you do not answer."

And were you really abandoned, Jesus? Or were you feeling something else? The gulf between head and heart that widens during pain—when we struggle to feel what we believe to be true?

"For he has not ignored or belittled the suffering of the needy," he continues. "He has not turned his back on them, but has listened to their cries for help."

God hadn't ignored you—you were sure of that. He had heard your cry, no matter what you felt. God may have been silent, but he was never absent.

Here is One who cried and bled in body, mind, and soul. Even at death he had no rest, with a jeering crowd and people plundering his clothes. And yet here is One who entrusted his life to a God who promised redemption. He breathed his last and bowed his head.

And he died—our sins on his shoulders.

I've always wondered what Easter Saturday was like, Lord. What were they preaching about in the synagogues that morning? Was it about you? What were they saying? And what did Mary and the apostles do? I imagine them huddled together, rocking back and forth on their chairs, dabbing their sunken eyes, filled with grief and guilt and disillusionment, while people outside went about life as usual—talking and eating, the children laughing as they chase the street dogs down the road. If you were the One your followers thought you were, things shouldn't have ended this way. But they had. And now all was silent. Their dreams were over.

"So he went and preached to the spirits in prison—those who disobeyed God long ago . . ."[6]

Whatever that verse means, it means all was not as those grieving followers thought. All was not silent. All was not over. You were active, moving—preaching. Like Job, they knew nothing of the heavenly drama that was unfolding. And they never expected what was to come.

Because here is One who took all by surprise—believer and villain alike. While some still sneered, he folded his grave clothes. While others still mourned, he walked from the tomb's door. Death hadn't been the end. His cry *had* been heard—the silence of Easter Saturday broken by the roar of his resurrection.

And here he stands now, looming above me, with his outstretched arms and golden heart. It's a white Jesus I see, his nose more European than Israeli; like any representation, this mosaic has its flaws. But while the details are wanting, it captures his essence well, pointing me to the real, unseen Jesus I worship in my soul. Here is One who is Lord of all, standing radiant, luminous, and worthy.

My journal is with me, and I write:

Bring your accusations . . . every accusation that could be leveled at a man: selfish, brutish, arrogant, ignorant, proud, racist, sexist, rude, imprudent, indulgent, negligent, lustful, disruptor of the peace for change's sake or acquiescent to the status quo.

None could be said of him. None of them will stick.

Try and find another worthy of worship.

Try and find one.

He never sinned, but he died for sinners to bring you safely home to God.[7]

Your suffering wasn't for nothing, Jesus. It brought us forgiveness and life. There was purpose to your pain.

"For God called you to do good, even if it means suffering, just as Christ suffered for you. He is your example, and you must follow in his steps."[8]

We gave you our lives years ago, Lord. Shall we take them back when things get difficult? Renege on the deal? Not accept the bitter with the sweet? Achieve your purposes through our pain.

I get up from the pew, walk back up the aisle, and find Merryn in a row of seats nearby. She's been praying too—praying for me.

Praying that God will give me my own new life.

*

Merryn and I climb the stairs to our fourth-floor apartment on Rue Rodier. The day had begun with coffee and crêpes, a Metro ride, and a walk around the Left Bank. Then we'd strolled across the Pont des Arts Bridge, past those little locks with their romantic wishes, to spend the rest of the day at the Louvre Museum. There we'd seen more of the world's treasures—da Vinci's *Mona Lisa*, Veronese's *The Wedding at Cana*, Delacroix's *Liberty Leading the People*, and sculptures like the *Venus de Milo*, Michelangelo's *The Dying Slave* and *The Rebellious Slave*, and Canova's *Psyche Revived by Cupid's Kiss*. This last piece had been particularly elegant. Psyche rests in Cupid's arms just moments after he's been scratched by his own arrow and fallen in love with her.

It's been a good day. It's been a special week. Tomorrow we'll have one last breakfast of coffee and crêpes, then leave the city of love for home.

"Fifteen years," she says, taking off her shoes.

"And never a cross word," I say, locking the door.

Merryn heads to the bathroom to get ready for bed. She brushes her teeth, removes her contact lenses, slips into her nightie and then between the sheets. When I think I've got her eye, I pull off my shirt and break into a faux model's pose.

"You know I can't see what you're doing without my glasses," she says sardonically.

"I'm showing you my six-pack," I say, hoping the rippling muscles of my taut abdominals prompt Cupid to shoot some arrows.

"Honey," she says, "these days your six-pack comes in a padded cooler bag."

Cupid steps aside and Gelos, the god of laughter, shoots us both instead.

Cupid, Gelos—enlightened souls like us tend to think we've left the myths behind. But like those rippling abdominals that others don't see, most of us hold to a few fairy tales. Like romance without sacrifice, friendship without difficulty, Christianity without adversity, and life without suffering. We all know that love rests at the core of life, but modern myths abound of a love based on wishes alone rather than promises, pledges, and vows.

But thank God for God.

And thank God for Jesus.

I thank Jesus for Merryn and the family of faith.

And for eternal love that's committed.

8

Positively Crucified

November 2011

A twenty-something mum pushes her stroller past my window. She wears the same simple outfit most days of the week—blue jeans, dark coat, black shoes, a hair clip. I bumped into her, literally, at the corner store once. She seemed friendly. She is one of a cast of characters I see daily from the study of our flat on Abingdon Road.

An older gent with a gentle face, blue collared shirt, and neatly combed hair passes twice each day, his aging Norwich terrier waddling behind him. An Indian lady in a faded sari is in the allotments across the road most afternoons tending her vegetable garden. A young guy with orange hair walks past with his rainbow-colored umbrella, and a few times a week an old man on a red mobility scooter zips down the footpath, his mouth wide open like a *Herman* cartoon character.

Many cycle past my window too, and hundreds more race past in their cars. But apart from the odd van or bicycle rider, it's the walkers I've come to recognize. Without them knowing it, they've become a part of my life as I observe their daily routines.

My desk tucks neatly into the box window that juts from the second floor of our house, giving a view to my right as well as one in front of me. As I sit writing, I notice someone approach our front door below from the corner of my eye.

Ding-dong.

Merryn opens the door before I make it downstairs. It's Ben, our next door neighbor, standing on the step with a wrapped-up bundle in his arms.

"I thought you'd like to meet this little guy," he says.

✻

"We've called him Tristan," Ben says, sitting down on the couch, his newborn curled against his chest. "Amanda's doing well, although the birth was quite difficult. She's home now, resting."

"Can I have a hold?" Merryn says.

Ben passes Tristan over and Merryn cradles him carefully.

"Don't you have a lot of hair," she says to the infant, stroking his head. "And don't you have such soft skin." Tristan gurgles and opens his eyes a little.

———

"Hello, little Tristan," I say, leaning toward him. "I'm your favorite uncle Sheridan." I try and claim this title with all the children I'm close to. Being the only Sheridan they're likely to know, I figure I may as well be their favorite one. "Now repeat after me: 'Hello, favorite uncle Sheridan . . .'"

"You do realize he's only four days old." Ben laughs.

"Early and often," I reply, "—that's my educational strategy."

Apart from a whimper now and then, Tristan rests contentedly in Merryn's arms while Ben tells us about their dash to the hospital a few nights ago for the delivery. It's good to see Merryn happily holding a baby. To me it speaks of her progress adjusting to our situation.

We'll get to know Tristan more in the weeks to come, and Ben and Amanda better as they struggle with baby flu and sleepless nights and even camp in our lounge room when their heating busts midwinter. And soon Amanda will join the cast of characters I see from my study each day, leaving her door to push Tristan in his pram around the neighborhood.

Ben soon takes his little bundle home, leaving us a box of chocolates as a gift. I return to the lounge to watch the news, and Merryn starts making dinner. A few minutes later I hear a faint noise coming from the kitchen. I walk in and find Merryn sniffing, dabbing her eyes with a tissue.

There is nothing to say. I just hold her.

"I thought I was doing better," she says.

"It will probably always hurt a little."

"I guess so."

Merryn takes her box of tissues through to the lounge room

and opens the box of chocolates. Ben wouldn't have known how handy his gift would be. Who doesn't find comfort in a little chocolate now and then.

"Do you think," she says, a few tissues later, "we should consider adopting here?"

"And start the process all over again?" I say, concerned where the conversation is heading. "The stressful application, the lengthy wait? We've made so much progress. I don't think I can face all that again."

"No," Merryn says with a sigh. "I probably can't either."

I hold her again and we each take another chocolate.

"In that case," she says, "I want something else."

"What?"

"A puppy."

"Me too," I say, and we laugh.

"What should we call him?"

"It needs to be a good English name," I say. "How about Rupert?"

"Or Reginald?"

"And he needs to be a scruffy dog. Let's call him Rupert Reginald McScruffy."

"We could get him christened at the Cathedral," Merryn jokes.

"He'd probably pee on the baptismal font and slurp the holy water."

"We'll need to move house to get a dog," she says, "since the landlord won't let us have one here. Maybe it's time to think about buying our own place."

"If we're sure we want to stay," I say, "and truly make England home."

Merryn takes one last chocolate, then closes the box, gets up from the couch, and starts walking back to the kitchen.

"What if it's a girl dog?" she says from the hallway.

"Then we'll call her Rupette."

And she smiles.

*

The blind will see, the deaf will hear, the lame will leap like a deer. In heaven, we're told, everything lost will reappear. Our youthful abilities and faculties will return. Lost loved ones in Jesus will be brought to our side. Even our pets could be there, wagging their tales with sticks in their mouths and games of fetch in their eyes.

But what of the childless couple who never "lost" because they never "had"? Will they be given a child? Jesus said there is no marriage in heaven—or no new marriages at least. So, no new births either? Will the single and childless miss out in heaven too?

*

The rising sun has begun to turn the icy silver allotments to green. Wisps of steam hover above a glowing River Thames, and rowers slice their oars through its liquid gold. The spires of Christ Church are beginning to glow, and the crispy frost on its manicured lawns is melting. Puddles of last night's rain flip the city on its head, Oxford's streets now filled with mirrors.

We take the Ring Road north and join the highway. With hours of driving ahead, we get some music playing. New Order, Roxy Music, U2, Florence and the Machine—it soon dawns on us that most of the music we've always liked is by British bands.

While we pass big cities like Birmingham and Manchester, for much of our journey we drive through countryside—past green rolling hills like softly ruffled blankets and yellow fields striped with tractor trails and dotted with bales of hay. An hour later we leave the freeway for narrow roads through rural towns with pubs with names like The Ol Stone Troigh and main streets with little corner stores, post offices, and parish notice boards. Soon the roads are lined with waist-high hedges to keep flocks of sheep from harm, and further still those hedges turn to dry stone walls that separate paddocks into pieces like a giant jigsaw puzzle. After a series of rises and dips, the trees thin out and we find ourselves in a valley of sky and fields. And after crossing a stone bridge over a gentle stream, we enter the North Yorkshire town of Kettlewell. We drive slowly through the village, turn at the King's Head pub, park the car in the lane, walk up the little driveway, and knock on the front door.

"Hello, Sheridan," says the tall man with a round belly and friendly face who greets us.

"Hello, Adrian," I say. "This is my wife, Merryn. Merryn, please meet Adrian Plass."

---

*

"Do you like our tea set?" Adrian says.

We sit in a bright lounge room with big windows, an open fire, and a border collie named Lucy, who coaxes me to play tug with a piece of rope. Bridget, Adrian's wife, has just laid a tray of tea and biscuits on the coffee table. Merryn and I look at the teapot with its four matching cups. They are all canary yellow with splotches of red, blue, and orange as if applied from a spray can. I pause for a moment, searching for the right words.

"It's, err, cheerful," I say.

"It's ghastly," says Bridget. "I don't know what we were thinking when we bought it."

"It looked pretty in the shop," Adrian says.

"Oh, thank goodness for that," Merryn says.

"You looked lost for words there, Sheridan," Adrian laughs.

Much of the next couple of hours is filled with laughter. We laugh at ourselves, our lives, and life in general as we get to know each other. Adrian drops a few of his famous anagrams into the conversation. ("Did you know that Anglican is an anagram of Gin Canal?" "I take great comfort in the knowledge that Fundamentalist is an anagram of I'm a Stunted Flan.") And we find Bridget rivals her husband for wit. ("I lined up for prayer at a healing meeting once, until waiting in line gave me a bad back.") We talk about our move to the UK and they talk about Scargill House—the retreat center they've helped to resurrect. A tray of sandwiches comes out, and Merryn and I feel like we've known our hosts for years—enjoying the warmth of a couple with remarkable gifts of hospitality and encouragement.

"We've booked dinner for 7:00 p.m.," Adrian says. "Would you like to go for a drive beforehand?"

"There's a place called Malham Cove we thought you might like to see," Bridget adds.

Merryn and I reach for our coats, and as we stand to leave I remark on a large framed picture on the wall of a beautiful tree in the snow.

"What a wonderful photograph," I say.

"Until you see the dog droppings," Adrian says.

I look closer at the picture. "You mean that little thing near the fence post?"

"A bit analogous to life really." Bridget laughs. "There's dog poo amongst the beauty."

＊

At eighty meters high and three hundred meters wide, Malham Cove looks like a giant waterfall that has run dry. Water did plunge from its peak eons ago, but today it is even more extraordinary. In what looks like a miraculous occurrence, a stream flows from the base of the cliff. The water comes, in fact, from deep caves underneath and emerges through a slit in the rock, but the effect is magical. Water streams down the valley from the cove as if Moses has struck it with his staff.

A rocky path and a series of stairs wind up the hill to the

cliff top. After enjoying its views, Merryn and I descend and find Adrian and Bridget by the stream, Adrian reclining on the slope.

"I was just having a pray," Adrian says, getting up.

"You fell asleep," Bridget says.

"I prefer to call it deep contemplation."

We walk down the path along the stream on our way back to the car. Merryn and Bridget walk ahead while Adrian and I trail behind.

"I was sorry to hear what you'd been through when we spoke last year," Adrian says. "How are you both doing now?"

"On the whole," I say, "we're a lot better. Coming to the UK has been the new beginning Merryn needed. My future is still up in the air, and Merryn still feels the loss at times, but I guess we're trying to focus on the upside of being childless and the opportunities it brings."

"Yes," he says, "although that can only take you so far."

We walk a little farther before Adrian explains what he means.

"We ran a retreat at Scargill House this year," he says. "We called it 'Positively Single'. The aim was to help single people feel better about their situation—to look at the upside, as you put it— and how they have more time, freedom, opportunity to travel, and things like that. Well, as soon as the first participants arrived on Friday night, it was clear they weren't feeling very positive about their singleness, no matter what opportunities it brought.

"I was scheduled to preach at the church service that week- end and decided to speak about Jesus hanging on the cross. I called the talk 'Positively Crucified?'. You see, no matter how hard we try, we cannot put a positive spin on the crucifixion.

It was a dark, barbaric event—there was no upside. And Jesus didn't try to find one. Instead, he did something else entirely."

"Go on," I say.

"Have you ever noticed how many people Jesus ministered to as he hung on the cross?" Adrian continues. "He ministered to his mother—"

"You mean, putting her in John's care?" I clarify.[1]

"That's right. And he ministered to the thief crucified next to him—"

"Who asked Jesus to remember him," I say, tracking along.[2]

"He ministered to the people who crucified him—"

"'Father, forgive them, for they don't know what they're doing.'"[3]

"He ministered to the Roman centurion—"

"Who came to believe in him."[4]

"And he ministered to us," Adrian says, "forgiving our sins through his sacrifice. All of this was done in the middle of his suffering, before things came good at his resurrection."

We walk through a gate in a dry stone wall and turn onto the road toward the car.

"My message to those singles that Sunday morning was this," Adrian says: "Yes, there may be some benefits in being single, but you will also find it difficult and lonely. Some days it will feel unbearable. But out of your suffering will come opportunities to minister to people in ways you otherwise never could.

"With Jesus, crucifixion is a mission field. Or, to put it another way, the fruit of suffering can be service."

———

*

"What about you, Merryn," Bridget says. "What are your dreams?"

Bridget, Adrian, Merryn, and I sit in a cozy nook of the Racehorses pub. Our main courses have just arrived—pork belly, chicken breast, Yorkshire puddings, a bottle of wine—as I've finished sharing some of my future career possibilities.

"I've come to realize," Merryn says after a pause, "that I can't have my dream."

There's a moment of empathic silence around the table, then Merryn shares the story that our dinner companions only know in outline—the story of our wilderness journey, our Christmas tragedy, and our move to England to start again. Sometimes shocked, often saddened, Adrian and Bridget acknowledge the pain without trying to fix or explain it. In a strange way, recounting the story in such an atmosphere is, itself, healing.

A few more laughs and a few tears later, we walk back home to the Plass's place. Bridget goes to bed and Merryn bids goodnight, leaving Adrian and me in the fire-lit lounge room with glasses of port. I ask Adrian about his books and his success in publishing. We talk about my book and my lack of a "profile." Then Adrian says something I'm not expecting.

"Have you considered writing your story into a book?" he says.

"What do you mean?" I say.

"Your story—everything you told us tonight."

"You mean, like a memoir?"

"Yes."

"Well, no, I . . ."

"I think it could help a lot of people."

A flurry of thoughts swirl as I ponder Adrian's suggestion. I'd never contemplated writing about our experience, and my mind soon fills with objections.

"I'm not sure I'm qualified to write a book about infertility."

"Your story isn't just about infertility," he says. "It's about broken dreams, tested faith, and the need for a new beginning. It's about taking a risk and starting again. It's about holding on to God when you don't understand him. I think many could benefit from reading about that."

"What about *More Than This*?" I say. "I've been working on it for months now."

"This could be a better book to release first. But it's entirely up to you."

Our conversation drifts to other things, but Adrian's idea won't leave me. I end up spiraling back to it later.

"This suggestion of yours—there's something Merryn and I would need to consider before I wrote such a book."

"What's that?"

"Whether we really want to share our story publicly. This is a very personal experience."

"You'll feel vulnerable at times," Adrian says. "You'll both need to think about that."

"One thing's for sure though," I say.

Adrian looks at me, listening.

"*Resurrection Year* would be a good title for such a book."

"Yes," he says, "it would."

———

December 25, 2011

A little snow fell overnight, so we sloshed our way through sleet to church. Merryn cooked a roast lamb for lunch, then we opened the hamper Mum and Dad sent. It was full of ham, fruit, biscuits, chocolates, cashews, sweets, and . . . a Christmas pudding. The last time we wanted one of those we left the supermarket with a packet of mince pies instead. What a different Christmas this has been. We thanked God for that tonight.

We spent the afternoon reading books—pure indulgence. Mine was The Great Divorce by C. S. Lewis. He has this scene at the end where a radiant lady is honored in heaven with a procession of singing girls and boys.

"And who are all these young men and women on each side?" the narrator asks his guide.

"They are her sons and daughters," the guide says.

"She must have had a very large family, Sir."

And the guide explains that, no, she didn't have a large family, but because she loved well on earth, every young man or boy that met her became her "son" in heaven—"even if it was only the boy that brought the meat to her back door"—and every girl she met became her "daughter."⁵

January 2012

"Remember that thing Charlotte used to say when she didn't get her way?"

Merryn and I sit in church after the morning service. Her

comment refers to a time when our niece, then two years old, wanted to play with *all* her blankets instead of just one, and the response she gave her mother when told she couldn't.

"When she said, 'You're ruining me!'?"

"In many ways I've been saying the same thing to God about having a child," Merryn says. "I've said, 'I want one. Why can't I have one? You're ruining me for not giving me one!' It's time for this to stop."

Merryn doesn't speak with teary angst or steely resolve but with the peace of one who has been whispered to by God. I sense a quiet breakthrough happening.

"To a two-year-old who sees only the present moment," she says, "having all your blankets to play with at once seems very important. In the grand scheme of things, of course, it's not. Having a child has seemed very important to me too. But in the grand scheme of eternity, perhaps it's not.

"I don't understand why God has said no to us having a child. Perhaps I never will. But I know him, and I know he wouldn't have meant this for evil. So it's time to let go of the why questions now.

"It's time for me to move on."

*

The Indian lady in her faded sari is out early in the allotments this morning. That older gent with the gentle face has just passed by with his terrier. The orange-haired guy clutches his rainbow umbrella, and that twenty-something mum walks by with her stroller. By the time Amanda takes Tristan out in his pram, I'm almost ready to write.

This is either an act of faith or lunacy, I say to myself.

It is fear I feel. Trepidation. And deep feelings of doubt. The fear felt is a fear of failure—of investing effort in a project that will never float. The trepidation is over what lies ahead— the memories I'll need to recall and retread. And the doubt is a doubt of my ability to write—attempting a genre I've never tried. So I pray again and take a breath.

And I stretch out my hands to type.

Rain falls like a thousand bullets,

I write,

a barrage of heavy drops pounding the roof, the hood, the asphalt . . .

I've spent the past two weeks reading piles of my old journals—reliving ten years of our lives through those coffee-stained pages. The words have evoked memories, and the memories, emotions. Some days Merryn has found me lost in joy, and other days in the darkest depths.

Don't think, just drive.

I type.

Turn the music up. No silence . . .

It was a surprise to me, but after thought and prayer Merryn had taken the vulnerable step of blessing Adrian's idea. And with little piles of notes covering our dining room table, we'd sketched out the stories each chapter should include. Stories like driving home to Sydney on Christmas Eve and stopping by a lonely motel. Stories like Merryn collapsing on the motel bed and my heart breaking into a thousand pieces.

God, this is cruel,

I write—

leaving us in this wilderness . . .

I know she'll struggle to read these words I type. I struggle to write them.

One minute we've glimpsed the promised land and the next minute you've barred us from entering it . . .

But maybe, just maybe, this story will help others.

Maybe the fruit of our suffering will come bound in a book.

February 2012

Leave all this and you start from scratch.

I write.

If you give up the show you can't get it back.

March 2012

Up into the clouds we fly,

I type,

before breaking through the misty pillow to the infinite blue beyond.

April 2012

And after a couple of months sitting at my desk with the cast of Abingdon Road by my window, I send a few pages of our story to some publishers.

*

"You're winning me over," she says as we lunch in a London restaurant. "This book has a lot of potential. We're interested."

*

"We talk a lot about the healing of pain," he says from his high-rise office, "but not a lot about the *redemption* of it. I'll be interested to read more."

*

"Most books like this end in a miracle," says another, "but that's not most people's experience. I'll be recommending *Resurrection Year* to our publishing board next month."

May 2012

The old man on the red mobility scooter zips down the footpath once more, his mouth again wide open. I wonder how it's not full of flies. I return from this diversion and write another sentence, then an e-mail icon flashes on my screen. It's from one of those keen publishers.

Dear Sheridan,
    We reviewed your book at our publishing board meeting yesterday.

And?

We think you write well and are interested in working with you.

Exciting!

However . . .

Oh?

. . . after some discussion we concluded that although you are well known in Australia, your profile here in the UK and in the States is slight, and we would struggle to sell your memoir . . .

And I don't manage much writing for the rest of the day.

*

A mother and child walk into the park, their enthusiastic Labrador straining on his leash. They settle across the pond from where I sit and watch the ducks, swans, and geese. At the other end of the pond three grandfathers race model boats. I watch them steer their craft around two white markers, wondering if the warship or the tug boat is ahead on laps, before being startled by a surge of barking and squawks.

Mother and child are now feeding bread to the ducks, drawing every feathered creature from far and wide. A flock of seagulls hovers overhead, squawking and swooping for each crumb of bread, and it is them that have the Labrador so excited. Now off his leash, he chases after the birds, dashing left and right in a figure-eight pattern. He jumps and barks, his tail madly wagging, rushing to and fro after his prey.

But then I notice something. While the seagulls are clearly the Labrador's concern, for the most part he faces away from them. His nose is on the path, not pointed to the sky; he barks at the hedge and not the pond. And then I realize what is happening.

The dog doesn't chase the seagulls themselves but their grey, fluttery shadows. He barks and jumps at those dancing illusions while the real thing lies elsewhere.

It's nearly twelve months since we left Sydney, I ponder. *By the calendar, our "Resurrection Year" is almost done. And where am I? I've spent a year writing two incomplete books that have no certainty of being published.*

Maybe I'm the one chasing shadows.

✳

"The Lord has given me a word for you," he says. "May I pray for you?"

Another Sunday morning in church. As it happens, I'm sitting next to Simon, the guy with the blond-grey hair who once addressed me from the stage. I accept his offer of prayer.

"God's word for you is *metamorphosis*," he says. "God is changing you into someone new."

Simon then prays for that change to happen, and for a sense of peace during the transition.

✳

"I'll let you two have a look upstairs," the agent says. "I'll be here if you have any questions."

We climb the stairs to the second floor with its two small bedrooms and bathroom. I've always wanted to live in a terrace house. They feel so playful—like an oversized children's cubby or doll's house. With its little blue door and odd little nooks, this one feels just like that. We look around the rooms and out the little windows to the backyard, letting our imaginations have a play.

"Just so you know," the agent calls from below, "council permission has already been granted to convert the loft into a third bedroom."

"That could be my studio," I say quietly to Merryn, not wanting the agent to hear I'm keen. "I can hear the show intro now: '*Live from the Loft* with Sheridan Voysey.'"

"Um, that would be our bedroom," Merryn corrects me. "This could be your study-studio right here." She points to the small spare room with a sloping floor.

"But I had this one in mind for Rupert."

"Will you tuck him into bed each night with a hot water bottle too?"

"Of course not," I say. "This will be his play room. He'll sleep in our bed with us."

Merryn laughs and we take the stairs back down to the lounge room. Though small, the main living area is bright and made all the more cheery by the toys and children's books on its shelves and the row of small bicycle helmets on the wall.

"Three little ones," the agent says, following our gaze to the helmets. "No wonder the owners want more space."

We clarify the price and thank the agent for her time.
And hope the bank manager sees the possibilities too.

✳

"The wilderness," I wrote on that fateful Christmas Eve.

A *wilderness* experience is what our journey had been.

I'd drawn the imagery, of course, from that momentous biblical story where the Jews set out for the promised land after their liberation from slavery. What started as an adventure for them had soon become an ordeal, with an eleven-day trek becoming forty years of wandering.

But as I sit this morning surveying Abingdon Road, a coffee in my hand before another day of writing, I'm intrigued by this little phrase. *The wilderness.* I reach for the big book on my left with the well-worn pages and read through the story again.

The wilderness, I find, reflecting on those scriptures, is a place of rich significance. At its best, it is the place where we encounter God and discover his will for our lives—like the Jews as they saw God in a pillar of cloud and fire and heard his thundering commands on Mount Sinai. At its worst, it is the place of unfaithfulness and judgment—where the people bowed to golden calves and walked in circles instead of forward.[6] And between these two themes lie a variety of others that mirror our everyday experience.

The wilderness is a place of trial, a place of doubt, a place of restless discontent. It's a place of blazing sun and barren ground, of wild animals and dark powers, where you feel vulnerable and exposed and fear your needs won't be met. It's a place of hardship and difficulty, where you question God's goodness in your adversity. It's a place of rootlessness and weariness where you search but can't find home.

A place of trial.

"I'm sorry, but it's negative again," says the nurse . . .

A place of doubt.

Or maybe God is just mean . . .

A place of restlessness.

I feel like I'll always be condemned to being restless and discontent, wanting to be somewhere else without knowing where that somewhere else is . . .

But while the wilderness is a place of struggle and pain, it is more than this, I find. While a place of trial, it is also a place of provision; while a place of doubt, it is also a place of discovery; while a place of restlessness, it is also a place of change. Because the wilderness, for the Jews, was a place of manna and quail coming down from heaven and clothes that never wore out. It was the place where they discovered their identity as Israel, the children of God, and the place where God changed their grumbling, wayward hearts.

A place of provision.

Honey, we're going to Oxford!

A place of discovery.

I am a child of God whether applauded or forgotten . . .

A place of change.

"God's word for you is metamorphosis."

The wilderness is a place of trial, of doubt, of restless

---

discontent; a place of provision, of discovery, of change. And as I rustle through those well-worn pages one more time, there is something else about the wilderness I find.

It is a place of transition.

Because the wilderness is the ground between what was and what will be—the place between slavery and freedom, between immaturity and wisdom, between God's promise and its fulfillment, between who we were and who we are to be. In the wilderness we become people we could never have become before moving into the next phase of our lives.

After forty years in the wilderness, the Jews entered the promised land.

After forty days in the wilderness, Jesus launched his world-changing mission.

And this gives me hope as I look out over Abingdon Road.

After the wilderness comes a new beginning.

June 2012

Dear Sheridan,

Oh, an e-mail from that big US publisher. Not that I stand much of a chance . . .

Thank you for your patience while we analyzed your book proposal.

All rejection letters start politely. I won't get excited.

———

Your story is quite moving. Both our editorial and publishing board members felt the same way.

Uh-huh. And there's a "but" coming, right?

I wish I could say books like this were easy to sell but,
unfortunately, they are not.

Thought so.

That said, your writing is engaging, personal, and inspiring.

Just say it—you don't want to publish my book.

We would be honored to publish your book.

And I go weak at the knees and have to lie down.

September 2012

The children's books are gone. There are no more toys on
the shelves. The row of bicycle helmets has been taken down,
and there are holes in the wall where the baby gate guarded the
stairs. The colorful crates in the spare room holding little shirts
and jumpers are gone, and there are no more rubber ducks on
the bathroom ledge. The rugs have been pulled up, the family portraits taken down, the previous owners have left, and
Merryn and I stand in our new Oxford home.

Our new, empty home.

There will be no bath time bubbles or giggles here anymore. No chasing butterflies in the yard or nursery rhymes before bed. There will be no playing dolls or Tonka trucks, no computer games or dress-ups; no sleepovers, birthday parties, cakes, wishes, or candles. There will be no lunch boxes, shiny shoes or first days at school, and no tummy aches, grazed knees, or ice cream remedies.

Just Merryn and me.

That means no fibs, tantrums, or truancy, of course. No broken curfews and sleepless nights, or clashes of will or schoolyard fights. But no high school graduations or university entrance letters either, or veils and ceremonies after bringing the boyfriend home for dinner.

But we're OK.

Merryn and I sit on the stairs, the front door key dangling from my hand. From here we look down on the lounge room area, and the spot in the corner where the television will stand. On that screen we'll see many Hollywood endings, where the dream comes true before the credits roll. In their own way, I guess, such fantasies point to heaven, where all the fragments are reconnected and the story ends well. But heaven isn't here yet. Not all dreams become reality.

And each day we adjust a little more to that truth.

The builders are due on Monday. Once they've finished the job of converting the loft, we'll start filling this vacant space. Our own picture frames will line those shelves—pictures of nephews, nieces, family, and friends, and a nice one of Riza from our second visit to the Philippines. Some of my photographs will line the walls—photos of Rome, Switzerland, and snow-covered Oxford taken during our year of resurrection. We'll carry boxes of good memories into that house on move-in day and fill it with new ones as the years roll on.

We'll fill this empty space with people soon too—for a combined house warming and fortieth birthday party. Ben and Amanda will come holding little Tristan, plus other new friends like Jeff and Ali and Simon with the blond-grey hair. This will come after a busy year of overseas guests who have already visited us on Abingdon Road—like Darren, my singer friend, who came for another stay with his family, and Louise, the Sydney pastor's wife, whose children proved most receptive to my favorite uncle Sheridan status. Bless them.

Will we be lonely in our forties? we worried all those years ago.

Some dreams may not come true, but most of our fears won't either.

I'll fill that spare room with the sloping floor with my desk, my books, and my photos, and I'll pray each morning for the gift of writing, and invitations to speak will start coming. (It's still my intention to have that loft for a studio, but let's keep that quiet for the time being.) Each night I'll tuck Rupert into his nice, warm bed—a little bed by the back door downstairs—and each week we'll thank God for our new life in England and the oversized doll's house we call home.

"Live overseas. Take a risk. Have an adventure," she'd said.

What an adventure our Resurrection Year has been.

We ask the One who encompasses the world to fill this empty house with his presence.

And make it a place of shared stories and healing.

✳

I turn the key on the little blue door, and Merryn and I get on our bicycles. We ride for a few minutes down Botley Road, then take a left onto the path along the Thames. Narrow boats are parked on the river's edge, their owners on fold-out chairs with glasses of wine. Families picnic on spread-out rugs, and kids mess about with fishing lines. Dogs chase ducks along the bank and amateurs zigzag haphazardly in punts. Sailing boats dodge and tack where the river widens out, their bulging sails harnessed to the wind.

We follow the path to the Godstow Lock, where boats line up to climb higher upstream, pass the remains of the old stone Abbey, and stop by the bridge to consider our journey. This path rolls on for miles and miles, following the bends of the River Thames and through fields and valleys and over hills. It winds and twists like a pencil line drawn by a giant hand.

Let's ride on a little farther, we decide.

The skies are blue and the sun is shining.

Acknowledgments

This was not the book I was expecting to write, but it seems to be the book I was *meant* to write. There were times when the writing process felt almost as difficult as living through the painful events it describes. At other times sentences fell into place as if given from above. The experience included both agony and joy, and I'm thankful for the following people who shared that experience with me.

Thank you, Merryn, my wife and soul mate, for taking the brave step of sharing our story with the world. I couldn't do what I do without you.

Thank you Adrian and Bridget Plass for that special weekend in November 2011 and subsequent weekends since. Without your timely words this book simply would not exist.

Thank you Peter Baade, Joanne Cox, Belinda Gor, Mike and Terasa Hardie, Heather Kelly, DJ and Louise Konz, Natalie

Lammas, Wendy Rayner, Sally Smith, and Kristy Voysey for laughing and crying along with some early chapters and providing helpful feedback.

Thank you Matt Baugher and the Thomas Nelson team for seeing something valuable in this story and bringing your expertise and excellence to its publication.

Thank you Ben Dawe for your invaluable publishing advice.

Thank you Philip Randal and the Hope Media team for the *Open House* memories.

Thank you Joanne Cox, Mal Fletcher, Rachel Green, Simon and Carol Jackman, Stephen and Bev Jones, Krish Kandiah, and Ben and Amanda Reed for helping us find our feet in the UK.

Thank you Steve and Louise Bartlett, the "Croydon Centre for Spiritual Enlightenment," and the many others who walked with us through the wilderness years.

Thank you Tony and Vivienne Voysey, my parents. No one prayed more during those difficult years, and for this book, than you both did.

And thank you God—thank you for new beginnings.

About the Author

Sheridan Voysey is a writer, speaker, and broadcaster on faith and spirituality. His books include the award-winning *Unseen Footprints: Encountering the Divine Along the Journey of Life*, and the three-volume series *Open House: Sheridan Voysey in Conversation*. He is married to Merryn and lives and travels from Oxford, United Kingdom.

To follow Sheridan and Merryn's continuing story, to share your own Resurrection Year, and for articles and podcasts on faith, spirituality, and new beginnings, please visit:
Sheridan's blog: www.sheridanvoysey.com
Facebook: www.facebook.com/sheridanvoysey
Twitter: @sheridanvoysey

Notes

Chapter 2

1. I tell a little more of my nightclub DJ story in chapter 2 of *Unseen Footprints: Encountering the Divine along the Journey of Life*, 2nd edition (Sydney, NSW: Strand, 2011).
2. I should quickly add that Family Radio grew in professionalism and is now the popular station 96five.

Chapter 4

1. See Genesis 1:2; Exodus 32:1–11; 35:30–36:1.

Chapter 5

1. The conversation that follows should not be read as a complete account of Greg Boyd's book or theology. See Gregory A Boyd, *Is God to Blame? Moving Beyond Pat Answers to the Problem of Suffering* (Downers Grove, Il: InterVarsity Press, 2003). Neither should it be read as a complete account of our own theological positions now. The conversation reflects our wrestling at the time.
2. Sean George's story is told in Sheridan Voysey, *Open House*

Volume 3 (Sydney, NSW: Strand Publishing, 2010), pages 170–180.

Chapter 7
1. Matthew 26:36–42 mentions Jesus frantically praying three times, seemingly without answer. Luke 22:43–44 mentions an angel appearing, but Jesus still prays "in anguish."
2. Matthew 26:39–42.
3. Mark 3:33–34.
4. See Isaiah 53:8, 10. The Messiah would die without biological descendants but have numerous spiritual descendants who benefit from his sacrificial ministry.
5. When Jesus cries, "My God, my God, why have you abandoned me?" he is quoting Psalm 22:1. No doubt he recited the entire psalm as he hung on the cross, and this is reflected in the following paragraphs.
6. See 1 Peter 3:18–20. One understanding of this cryptic verse is that, between his death and resurrection, Jesus preached to the spirits of Noah's contemporaries.
7. 1 Peter 3:18.
8. 1 Peter 2:21.

Chapter 8
1. John 19:26–27.
2. Luke 23:39–43.
3. Luke 23:33–34.
4. Luke 23:47; Matthew 27:54.
5. C. S. Lewis, *The Great Divorce* (Hammersmith, London: Harper Collins Publishers, 2002), 119.
6. The Jews' wilderness journey is recorded in Exodus 12:31–20:21 (from Egypt to Mount Sinai) and Numbers 10–36 (from Mount Sinai to Canaan, the Promised Land). Jesus retraced this path from Egypt to the wilderness before starting his mission to the world (Matthew 2:13–23; 4:1–7; Mark1:12–20; Luke 4:1–21). The details that follow are drawn from these references.